U   S   A   F   E

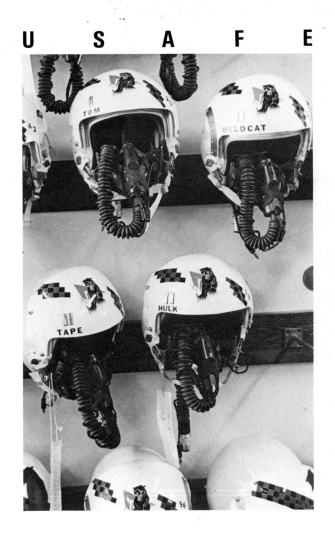

U · S · A · F · E

A Primer of Modern Air Combat in Europe

Michael Skinner
Photography by George Hall

Presidio Press ☆ Novato, California

To
Pat

Published by Presidio Press, 31 Pamaron Way, Novato, CA 94947.

Library of Congress Cataloging in Publication Data

Skinner, Michael, 1953–
    USAFE, primer of modern air combat.

    1. United States. Air Force. Air Forces in
Europe. 2. Air warfare. I. Title. II. Title:
U.S.A.F.E., a Primer of modern air combat.
UG633.S53   1983   358.4'00973   82-16479
ISBN 0-89141151-8

Design and Maps by Bill Yenne
Printed in Japan by Dai Nippon Printing Co., Ltd.

Half-title page

Monogrammed helmets await F-111 pilots at RAF Lakenheath.

Title page

Sparrow and Sidewinder air-to-air missiles about to be loaded onto Zulu Alert F-15s at Bitburg, Germany.

Facing title page

F-16 with long-range tanks refuels during trans-Atlantic delivery flight to Hahn, Germany.

Photographer's note:
All photographs were taken with Nikon F-3 and FE cameras, using a variety of lenses ranging from 15mm wide-angle to 600mm telephoto. Kodachrome-64 was used for the color shots, Ilford XP-1 for black and white. Aerial photos were taken during flights in the F-15 Eagle, the RF-4C Phantom, and the KC-10 and KC-135 tankers.

Contents

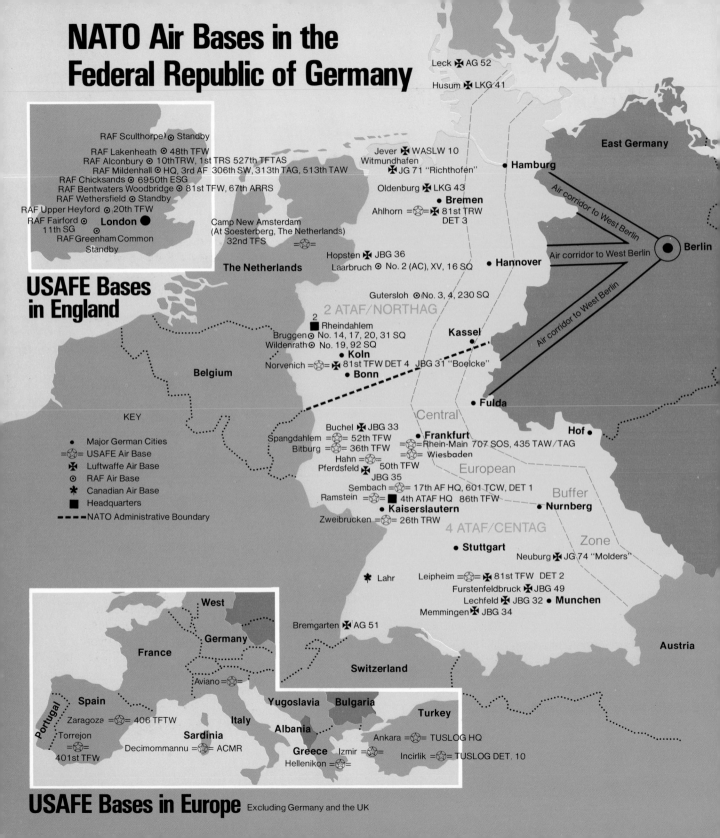

NATO Air Bases in the Federal Republic of Germany

Leck ✠ AG 52
Husum ✠ LKG 41

East Germany

RAF Sculthorpe ⊙ Standby
RAF Lakenheath ⊙ 48th TFW
RAF Alconbury ⊙ 10thTRW, 1st TRS 527th TFTAS
RAF Mildenhall ⊙ HQ, 3rd AF 306th SW, 313th TAG, 513th TAW
RAF Chicksands ⊙ 6950th ESG
RAF Bentwaters Woodbridge ⊙ 81st TFW, 67th ARRS
RAF Wethersfield ⊙ Standby
RAF Upper Heyford ⊙ 20th TFW
RAF Fairford ⊙
11th SG   **London** ●
RAF Greenham Common
Standby

Jever ✠ WASLW 10
Witmundhafen
✠ JG 71 "Richthofen"
Oldenburg ✠ LKG 43
Ahlhorn =⊙✠= 81st TRW
DET 3

● **Bremen**
● **Hamburg**

Camp New Amsterdam
(At Soesterberg, The Netherlands)
32nd TFS   =⊙=

Hopsten ✠ JBG 36
Laarbruch ⊙ No. 2 (AC), XV, 16 SQ

The Netherlands

● **Hannover**

Gutersloh ⊙ No. 3, 4, 230 SQ

USAFE Bases in England

2 ATAF/NORTHAG

2
■ Rheindahlem
Bruggen ⊙ No. 14, 17, 20, 31 SQ
Wildenrath ⊙ No. 19, 92 SQ
Norvenich =⊙✠= 81st TFW DET 4 JBG 31 "Boelcke"
● **Koln**
● **Bonn**

● **Kassel**

Air corridor to West Berlin
Air corridor to West Berlin
Air corridor to West Berlin
● **Berlin**

Belgium

KEY

● Major German Cities
=⊙= USAFE Air Base
✠ Luftwaffe Air Base
⊙ RAF Air Base
✱ Canadian Air Base
■ Headquarters
- - - NATO Administrative Boundary

● **Fulda**

Central

Buchel ✠ JBG 33
Spangdahlem =⊙= 52th TFW
Bitburg =⊙= 36th TFW   =⊙= Rhein-Main 707 SOS, 435 TAW/TAG
Hahn =⊙= 50th TFW   =⊙= Wiesbaden
Pferdsfeld =⊙=
JBG 35
Sembach =⊙= 17th AF HQ, 601 TCW, DET 1
Ramstein =⊙= ■ 4th ATAF HQ 86th TFW
● **Kaiserslautern**
Zweibrucken =⊙= 26th TRW

● **Frankfurt**

● **Hof**

European

Buffer

● **Nurnberg**

4 ATAF/CENTAG

Zone

● **Stuttgart**

Neuburg ✠ JG 74 "Molders"

✱ Lahr   Leipheim =⊙=✠ 81st TFW DET 2
Furstenfeldbruck ✠ JBG 49
Lechfeld ✠ JBG 32 ● **Munchen**
Memmingen ✠ JBG 34

Austria

Bremgarten ✠ AG 51

USAFE Bases in Europe Excluding Germany and the UK

**West
Germany**
France
Switzerland
Yugoslavia   **Bulgaria**
Italy   **Albania**   **Turkey**
Aviano =⊙=
Spain   **Sardinia**   **Greece**
Zaragoza =⊙= 406 TFTW
Torrejon
=⊙=   Decimommannu =⊙= ACMR
401st TFW
Portugal
Ankara =⊙= TUSLOG HQ
Izmir =⊙=   Incirlik =⊙= TUSLOG DET. 10
Hellenikon =⊙=

Acknowledgments

It is quite possible to write a book about aviation and never leave your living room—in fact, most works on the subject seem to have been written that way. But photographer George Hall and I wanted to breathe life into the technical jargon and dry statistics, to illustrate in words and pictures a clear story of America's air defense commitment to NATO.

We recently toured most of the major USAFE bases in Europe, photographing and interviewing countless pilots, technicians, and crewmen in Germany and in the United Kingdom. It is to these patient and courteous people that we owe our greatest thanks.

We would also like to thank Lt. Col. Eric Solander and Capt. Fran Tunstall of the USAF Books and Magazines Division in Washington, and Lt. Col. John H. Williams, chief of the USAFE Media Relations Division in Ramstein. Our "guides" in Europe were all gracious and generous with their time, but for service above and beyond the call of duty we would like to salute Sgt. Dave Jenkins (Ramstein), Mrs. Laura Overstreet (Bitburg), Lt. Deb Bossick (Spangdahlem), Capt. Ann Booth (Hahn), Lt. Rick Reisling (Sembach), Lt. Col. Fred Morgan (Mildenhall), Sgt. Mark Moore (Lakenheath), Capt. Mark Anderson (Alconbury), Capt. Kathy McCollom (Bentwaters), Maj. John Lehman (European Tanker Task Force Mildenhall), and, for some magnificent photo flights, Capt. Rich Sauter and his crew on "Balls 8," oldest and noblest tanker in the Ohio Air National Guard.

The author would also like to thank the staffs of the Library of Congress, the Air Force Systems Command Library at Andrews Air Force Base, and the library of the National Air and Space Museum for their kind assistance.

Although it is impossible to list every reference consulted in the writing of this book, special appreciation must be given to the following sources. The *USAF Fighter Weapons Review* is perhaps the best reference for the nitty-gritty of modern air combat and was the source of the Soviet article quoted in Chapter 8 (condensed by Lt. Rana Pennington). Much of the USAFE order of battle information was taken from "England's Americans" and "Europe's Americans," two excellent articles by Lindsay Peacock, published in the equally excellent *Air International* magazine. And, of course, every aviation writer pinches from the great Bill Gunston, who, it seems, writes a book a day before breakfast and has yet to write a bad one.

The manuscript was read by Mr. David Isby, author of *Jane's Weapons and Tactics of the Soviet Army,* Mr. John Prados, author of *The Soviet Estimate,* and various other aviation authorities and military personnel. All were gracious with their time and knowledge, but the author reserves responsibility for any mistakes or inaccuracies remaining in the text.

And for their contribution to one writer's education, the author owes a debt that can never be repaid to Mr. Larry Woods and Mr. Eugene Patterson.

1

Glossary

AAA: Antiaircraft artillery

AAFCE: Allied Air Forces Central Europe; parent command organization for all NATO air units in the central European theater. Headquartered in Ramstein, West Germany.

ACMR: Air Combat Maneuvering Range; sometimes more specifically called the ACMI (Air Combat Maneuvering Instrumentation) range, the ACMR is a weapons range monitored by electronic beacons that receive signals from special pods carried by aircraft taking part in the exercise. The signals are processed through a computer, which displays the mock air battle on huge, four-color video screens that accurately portray the relative positions and flight parameters of all pod-equipped aircraft.

ADC: Air Defense Command

ADV: Air Defense Variant; the British version of the Tornado optimized for air superiority missions.

AGE: Aerospace Ground Equipment; the portable gear, such as generators and test equipment, used in flight-line aircraft servicing.

AGS: Aircraft Generation Squadron; one of the three maintenance squadrons attached to every USAFE combat wing, the AGS is charged with flight-line support.

AIMVAL/ACEVAL: Air Intercept Missile Evaluation/Air Combat Evaluation; a series of operational tests conducted in the mid-seventies to determine the relative merits of competing USAF and Navy air-to-air missiles (AIMVAL) and later expanded to explore different theories of air combat (ACEVAL).

AMRAAM: Advanced Medium Range Air-to-Air Missile; USAF program to develop a replacement for AIM-7 Sparrow radar-directed missile.

AMU: Aircraft Maintenance Unit; one of the three sub-divisions of each AGS, each AMU is designated by the same squadron it supports—for example, the 22nd AMU would provide flight-line maintenance for the 22nd Tactical Fighter Squadron.

APG: Aircraft Personnel Group; more commonly referred to as "crew chiefs," the APG is responsible for coordinating flight-line maintenance and aircraft launching and recovery.

ARM: Anti-Radiation Missile; an air-to-surface missile designed to home in on the radiation emitted by hostile radar transmitters.

ASM: Air-to-Surface Missile

ASOC: Allied Sector Operations Center; NATO unit that directs defensive air operations.

ASRAAM: Advanced Short Range Air-to-Air Missile; USAF program to develop a replacement for the AIM-9 Sidewinder heat-seeking missile.

ATC: Air Training Command

ATOC: Allied Tactical Operations Center; NATO unit that directs offensive air operations

AWACS: Airborne Warning and Control System; theoretically any sophisticated airborne radar aircraft, the term is used almost exclusively to refer to the Boeing E-3A Sentry.

AX: Attacker Experimental; a USAF program begun in the mid-sixties to develop a dedicated close air support aircraft. The AX program culminated in the Fairchild A-10A Thunderbolt II.

BAOR: British Army of the Rhine

BIT: Built In Test; self-monitoring function designed into most modern avionic systems

BVR: Beyond Visual Range

CAP: Combat Air Patrol; usually combined with a prefix to denote a type of air combat mission—LOWCAP (low altitude fighter operations), RESCAP (protecting orbiting rescue helicopters and aircraft), and so on. The pilots' favorite is MIGCAP, which needs no further explanation.

CAS: Close Air Support

CBU: Cluster Bomb Unit

CENTAG: Central Army Group

CLAW: Concept of a Light Aerial Weapon; USAF candidate for an AIM-7 Sidewinder missile replacement, tested in AIMVAL.

CMO: Chief of Maintenance Operations; the wing administrator in charge of all aircraft maintenance and support. More often referred to as the Deputy Commander for Maintenance (DCM).

CO: Commanding Officer

CRT: Cathode Ray Tube; video display terminal

CV: Vice Commander

DACT: Dissimilar Air Combat Training

DASH-60: Portable generator unit used to start and provide ground power for certain aircraft.

DCM: Deputy Commander for Maintenance (see CMO)

Det: Detachment

DO: Deputy Commander for Operations; the wing commander's right-hand man, responsible for most day-to-day flying operations.

ECM: Electronic Countermeasures; the use of special equipment to defeat or lessen the effectiveness of enemy guidance and fire-control systems.

ETTF: European Tanker Task Force

EW: Electronic Warfare

EWO: Electronic Warfare Officer; second crewman in F-4G Wild Weasel.

FAC: Forward Air Control

FEBA: Forward Edge of Battle Area; in popular terms, the battlefield, or the front. Also called the FLOT (Front Line of Troops).

FMC: Fully Mission Capable

4 ATAF: Fourth Allied Tactical Air Force; command organization for all NATO air units in Central Europe south of the Bonn-Kassel line, including most USAFE combat air units. Headquartered at Ramstein, West Germany.

FX: Fighter Experimental; USAF program begun in the mid-sixties to develop an air superiority fighter. The FX program culminated in the McDonnell Douglas F-15 Eagle.

GCI: Ground Control Intercept

HAWK: Homing All the Way Killer; standard U.S. medium-range surface-to-air missile system.

HOTAS: Hands On Throttle And Stick

HUD: Head-Up Display; a clear video screen installed above the forward instrument panel in most modern aircraft displaying computer-generated navigation and weapons system information.

IFF: Identification, Friend or Foe; electronic devices designed to determine which unidentified aircraft are friendly and which are enemies.

I-HAWK: Improved HAWK (see HAWK)

INS: Inertial Navigation System

IR: Infrared

JAAT: Joint Air Attack Team; USAF and Army units working in concert to defeat an enemy armor attack.

JAWS: Joint Attack Weapons Systems; USAF/Army exercises to develop tactics for mutual support, culminating in JAAT.

KBO: *Kampfbeobachter* (German); Luftwaffe equivalent of WSO

LRU: Line Replaceable Unit

MAC: Military Airlift Command

MR: Mission Ready

NADGE: NATO Air Defense Ground Environment; an interlocking system of radar sites, command posts, fighters, surface-to-air missiles, and anti-aircraft guns.

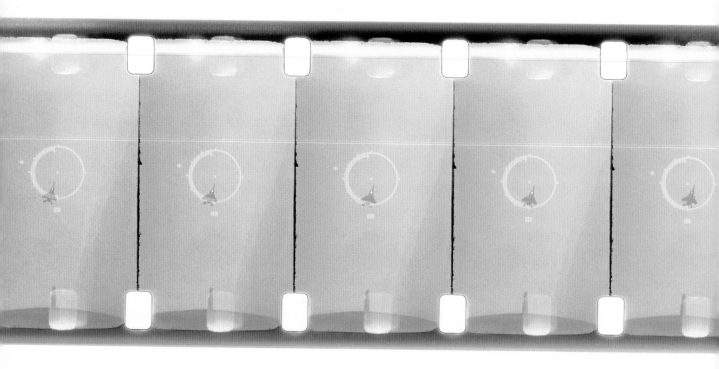

NATO: North Atlantic Treaty Organization

NFO: Naval Flight Officer

NORTHAG: Northern Army Group; a NATO command.

NOTAM: Notice To Airmen; posted advisories with information of interest to pilots concerning airport maintenance, traffic, etc.

OCU: Operational Conversion Unit

ODD RODS: NATO designation for a type of Soviet IFF system.

PAVE TACK: An all-weather laser weapons-delivery system currently being installed on some versions of the F-111 and F-4.

PGM: Precision Guided Munitions; popularly called "smart bombs."

QRA: Quick Reaction Alert

RAF: Royal Air Force; the air arm of the United Kingdom

RAFG: Royal Air Force, Germany

RF: Radio Frequency

RIO: Radar Intercept Officer; US Navy equivalent to WSO

Route Package (or Route Pack): One of seven areas of North Vietnam designated by the USAF for targeting air strikes.

RPV: Remotely Piloted Vehicle

SAC: Strategic Air Command

SALT: Strategic Arms Limitation Talks

SAM: Surface-to-Air Missile

SEAM: Sidewinder Expanded Acquisition Mode

2 ATAF: Second Allied Tactical Air Force; command organization for all NATO air units in Northern Central Europe. Peacetime headquarters at Rheindahlem, West Germany; wartime headquarters at Maastricht, Holland.

SIF: Selective Identification Feature

SW: Strategic Wing

TAB-V: Theater Air Base Vulnerability Shelter; a type of hardened aircraft shelter.

TACAN: Tactical Air Navigation; a navigation sys-

tem that locates an aircraft relative to an electronic beacon.

TADIL: Data-link language used by E-3A AWACS and ground units. Pronounced "TATTLE."

TDY: Temporary Duty

TFS: Tactical Fighter Squadron

TFW: Tactical Fighter Wing

TFX: Tactical Fighter Experimental; joint USAF/Navy program to develop a common strike aircraft. After much controversy and Navy withdrawal, the TFX program culminated in the F-111.

TISEO: Target Identification System, Electro-Optical; a stabilized video camera with a powerful zoom lens, mounted in the port wing of some F-4E's.

TOW: Tube-launched, Optically-tracked, Wire-guided; an antitank missile used by ground and helicopter forces.

TRA: Temporarily Reserved Airspace; a section of

sky cleared of all air traffic except the participants in a mock air battle.

UPT: Undergraduate Pilot Training

USAF: United States Air Force

USAFE: United States Air Forces in Europe

USEUCOM: The unified command that exercises command over all U.S. Army, Navy, and Air Force units in the European theater.

VID: Visual Identification; confirmed sighting and classification of an aircraft. Also called a "VIZ."

VTOL: Vertical Take-Off and Landing

WSO: Weapons System Operator; crewman in the second seat of an F-4.

5

Chapter 1
Introduction: Zulu Alert

Bitburg, West Germany. Zulu Alert.

The two-story industrial green building at the far end of the runway looks like a fire station. But when the horn goes off, pilots—not firemen—will slide down the poles. When the garage doors swing open, fighters—not fire engines—will scream out onto the asphalt. And they won't be on their way to put out a fire; the Zulu mission is to scramble, intercept, and—if necessary—shoot down intruders that wander across the buffer zone between West and East Germany.

If war ever came to Europe, the Zulu fighters would be the first planes to get into the fighting. It is serious business. The Zulu Alert shack is manned 24 hours a day, 365 days a year. The four F–15s are kept "cocked"—ready to fly and fight at any moment, loaded with fuel, armed with live missiles and gun ammo, their navigation systems all lined up.

"The Zulu fighters are the policemen of the sky," says one pilot. "We can be good or we can be bad. We can help an aircraft in distress. Maybe someone lost all his nav equipment and it's a bad weather day—we can be scrambled to help him come home."

Left: Pilot and crew chief rush to their Zulu Alert F-15 at Bitburg. The Zulu two-ship flight will start its take-off roll only three minutes after the alarm sounds.

Most of the Zulu scrambles are "Tango," or training missions. And almost all the "Alpha" scrambles—real live intercepts—wind up with the Zulu birds shepherding some hapless civilian pilot who has somehow strayed into restricted airspace.

Very rarely do combat aircraft from Eastern Europe violate the buffer zone. "You read in the papers anytime anything exciting happens," says one Zulu pilot at Bitburg. "And when's the last time you read anything exciting?" But another pilot allows, "They do stray across the border occasionally," and the pilots must be ready in case anything "exciting" does happen.

Zulu is the peacetime mission for Bitburg and the rest of the NATO fighter bases in Europe, part of the "Quick Reaction Alert." Every NATO combat air unit has a Quick Reaction Alert (QRA) commitment. Air defense units maintain a "QRA-India," an interceptor force like the Zulu flight, that can be scrambled on very short notice.

NATO strike units maintain a "Victor Alert," similar to Zulu Alert, but are never scrambled. The Victor Alert units have constant drills, but the aircraft rarely get past the concertina wire and electric fences of their "Special Weapons Area." Their QRA-Victor mission is simple: When the war starts they will spin the mountains of Eastern Europe into glass.

The Zulu pilots are regular line jocks and pull the alert duty about twice a month. They are always from the same squadron and usually from the same flight. As often as possible, the Zulu pilots are matched with their regular wingmen. The enlisted personnel stay on Zulu Alert for two days on and two days off. They do all the cooking and housekeeping, in addition to maintaining the four Zulu fighters.

The pilots muster at the squadron headquarters about seven-thirty in the morning to get their flight gear. They report to the Zulu shack around eight-thirty, although the official changeover takes place at nine, when the old crew take their gear out of the aircraft and the new crew put their stuff in.

The Zulu pilots dress for war. The colorful patches and unit insignia are stripped from their uniforms for security reasons. They wear their G-suits while on alert duty because they can't take the time to strap them on when the horn blows. The uncomfortable G-suits are removed around five o'clock, as soon as regulations allow. If they are scrambled after that they will fly without them.

The only classified material allowed in the Zulu shack is the little "yellow pages" of classified radio frequencies the pilots stash in the pockets of their flight suits. Since they can't bring any other classified material to study, they have to find other ways to occupy their time while waiting for the horn to go off.

There's a bunch of paperback mysteries on a shelf above the couch on the second floor of the Bitburg Alert building. The "good stuff" is stowed in a locker underneath a newly donated videotape player. There's also a dart board in the lounge, but the backboard has been extended recently because the pilots—America's first line of defense in central Europe, those eagle-eyed killers of the sky —kept missing the dart board completely and tearing big chunks out of the wall.

At night the Zulu crew watches movies. They get the same movies that come through the base theater, the same movies every American overseas base gets: B-movies, and a year late at that. Occasionally, however, they will get a real thriller,

and when the horn goes off at a particularly suspenseful point, they say you can scrape the pilots off the ceiling.

The pilots sleep in four summer camp–type bunks. The Zulu flight leader, who is always the highest ranking officer of the four pilots, sleeps in the same type of monkish cubicle as the other three pilots, but at least he has a telephone. There is also a small shower that is almost never used— the Zulu flight is rarely scrambled at night, and if it is, it is almost certainly not a drill. Pilots are a superstitious lot and are convinced that there's something about taking a shower in the Bitburg Zulu stall that makes people want to violate the sovereign airspace of the Federal Republic of Germany.

There is a small operations center facing the runway at the Bitburg Zulu shack, but it is rarely manned. On one wall there is a large flight map of the two Germanys, showing the restricted flying areas as well as the buffer zone along the border. The most popular attraction in the operations center is the "Doofer" book, an informal log kept by Zulu pilots. It records who was on duty, when they scrambled, and so forth. It is, in turns, funny, crude, catty, and always interesting. There is a drier, more formal version called the Battlelog, and a similar book at the runway control box, but the Zulu Doofer book is the funniest.

There is also a secure phone, but the Bitburg pilots prefer to eavesdrop on the "Tac Loop," the command circuit, hoping to get some advance warning on when they will be scrambled. Usually, they'll hear something is up and are almost ready to jump into their planes when the final order comes to "Scramble . . . Ramstein!" Arggh! Back to the dart board.

The two Bitburg Zulu flights never launch on the same training scramble. Neither are Bitburg and, say, Ramstein, scrambled at the same time. The pilots usually get "the words"—the scramble orders—before they're up in the air, when the

ground controllers tell them it's a Tango and vectors them against some other flight that's agreed to be intercepted for practice.

There are lots of restrictions concerning flying with live ordnance. The Tango scrambles are rather "vanilla" intercepts, just visual passes outside of weapons parameters. Even on an Alpha scramble, the Zulu pilots are very careful as to how they approach the "zombie."

"If it happened to be a hostile aircraft, we would definitely get the word down from higher headquarters specifically what we would be required to do," says a Zulu pilot. "We would not go right at him balls-to-the-wall and try to provoke anything."

The Zulu pilots never know what to expect. They spend most of their time waiting for the horn to go off, knowing full well it will blast when they least

Cocked and ready. A USAFE Eagle, armed to the teeth with Sidewinders and Sparrows, waits in its TAB-V hangar, ready to go at a moment's notice, whether the call to arms be just another drill or the long-dreaded Round Three.

expect it. And they can never be sure what's going to happen in the air, either. It could be just another training mission. Or it could be the bell that signals the start of Round Three.

It's this mixture of tension and tedium that makes the Zulu Alert a less than desirable duty to pull. As one Zulu pilot puts it: "It's twenty-four hours of boredom interrupted by five minutes of sheer terror."

Chapter 2
Air Superiority: The Contract

Ah, Bitburg! Fighter Pilot Heaven!

Floating alone in the perpetual central European overcast, the young pilot steals a few seconds to gloat at his triumph. After all, just about every would-be fighter jock fresh out of Undergraduate Pilot Training dutifully fills in his blue form with "F–15, F–16 *anywhere!*" But how many actually make it to the miracle jets? Damn few—and fewer still get all the way to USAFE. The handful of young tigers that show up at Bitburg each season consider themselves a lucky bunch indeed.

So who can begrudge the new pilot his brief celebration? He plows the clouds at the very top. Only the high canopy and the vertical tails poke through the muck; the rest of the plane is invisible. It is a feeling of weightlessness, of craftless flight through the German gray heavens (Home of Aces! Scene of Countless Combats!). Eventually he will be brought back to earth by the twin fins of reason and responsibility that shadow him like sharks across the sky. But not until he snatches a glimpse of life at the operational ceiling. It is as if the young pilot has set a course on Ulloa's Rind, the glorious rainbow of concentric circles known only to those who fly, and he—not his airplane, not that bat-winged marriage of titanium and technology—but he himself is hurtling through the heart of it. Bitburg! *Fighter Pilot Heaven! Dreams come true!*

This may seem an extraordinary fuss to make over what should be a routine assignment, but Air Force insiders know flying fighters in Europe is Big Time, an essential pit stop on the road to success. In the absence of combat, even proximity to danger counts. It is one thing to be "ace of the base" at MacDill or Langley, and quite another to be "Sierra Hotel" in Germany, with the Big Red Machine just twenty minutes away. (At Rosson, a Soviet bombing range, there is a target airfield that looks an awful lot like Bitburg AB.) To a young fighter jock, Vietnam is just a scary place the older pilots talk about. Europe is the new nest of future eagles, *the* place for ambitious young men to get their tickets punched and their air-squares filled. As a Bitburg squadron commander pronounced at a rather liquid celebration honoring his newest pilots' ascension to Mission Ready status, they are "at the very, very pointiest tip of the spear, facing the wily Russian horde over (he points vaguely to the east) in that direction."

There are two command hierarchies in the U.S. Air Force. The first is the institutionalized chain of command. It is a hierarchy of rank and organization—who salutes whom and what reports to what. You can diagram it on paper. You can look it up in countless manuals and organization charts, and it will make perfect sense. But it will give you a false feeling of understanding, because that's not the way the USAF works at all.

Left: Hahn-based F-16 high over typical German overcast. Instrument take-offs and landings are standard procedure in the often-grim weather of Central Europe.

11

The second hierarchy doesn't make sense, not to outsiders, but it is the reason why USAFE—"US Air Forces in Europe"—looks good on a pilot's resume. It is a hierarchy not of rank, but of class; of status, not grade. You will never find it written down, but in the Air Force the pilot is king. It is an oligarchy of the rated over the nonrated. Rank has little to do with it—the real pecking order is worked out in the sky and the more than half a million people in the USAF who never leave the ground are recognized only for their direct contribution to keeping the boys flying.

It is a pilot's world, but then there are pilots and there are fighter pilots—no MAC heavy drivers allowed. Fighter pilots will sometimes express, for the press, for the record, what a wonderful job those dedicated Military Airlift Command guys do

F-15s of Bitburg's 525th TFS join up in formation over Belgian practice area.

on their vitally important missions, but there is always a tip-off—a bored sigh perhaps, a wry twist of the jaw—that the "trash haulers" are, well, different. They exist in a different world, a world of "nineteen throttles and plastic spoons" and are not to be discussed on the same cassette with actual fighter pilots. The MAC pilots may get shot at, but they won't get to shoot back, and that makes all the difference. As it says on the T-shirt, "There are only two types of aircraft: Fighters and Targets."

The Air Force has a crush on the fighter pilot. (So does the Navy. They have a saying: "Never ask a pilot if he flies fighters. If he does, he'll tell you. If he doesn't, why embarrass him?") It is the romance of the single combat warrior, the intrepid knight of the air, grappling *mano a mano* with a numerically superior enemy, with only transcendent technology and his own cunning and skill to turn back the godless swarm. It is the fighter pilot mystique and it is a very real thing in the USAF. It decides who's hot and who's not; the fastest movers up the other, organizational, ladder will always have fighter time.

The Air Force, which helped create the myth, is now ruled by it. Some critics have claimed the cosmically complex F-15 should have had two crew members to handle the work load, but the romance of the single combat warrior held by those at the top quickly overruled the idea. Others say the USAF is not pursuing the extremely promising field of remotely piloted vehicles with the dispatch it deserves because of a reluctance to create a whole new generation of aircraft, no matter how capable, without a pilot on board.

In some cases, the Air Force has created a Frankenstein's monster with its fighter pilot fixation; and it comes back to haunt them when they hold out their hand on Capitol Hill and find Congress reluctant to fund anything but fighters.

Caught between admiration and jealousy, it's no wonder fighter pilots are a singularly schizoid lot. They are politely arrogant, benignly aggressive, and embrace democracy in the squadron with the zealous fervor that comes with knowing their superiority is never in question. They are individuals, yet interchangeable; regimented, yet independent. They can be sloppily sentimental one moment and coldly rational the next. The world of the fighter pilot is a world of contradictions. It is hostile territory for outsiders but a cozy community for those inside.

Fighter pilots use several methods to insulate themselves from regular earth people, the most important of which is language. Fighter pilots have their own vocabulary. Most of the words have to do with flying, of course, but a lot of them just *sound* operational and are actually code words for rather ordinary things and ideas. The most common fighter pilot expletive is "Sierra Hotel," meaning "shit hot" and denoting anything true, good, and useful to a fighter pilot. "Whiskey Delta" is just the opposite. A Whiskey Delta is a "weak dick," a man who just can't cut it, the worst thing you can call a fighter pilot.

There are countless euphemisms for the fighter pilots' favorite subject—destroying enemy aircraft in the sky. Fighter pilots never merely shoot someone down, they "hose" them, they "shoot their lips off" or "blow their shorts off." In written reports they may "pick up the enemy" and "put ordnance on him" or "convert a shot opportunity." But there is no jargon for the reciprocal action, the pilot's own death in the air. It is a forbidden topic, to be discussed only when absolutely necessary—in conversation with an outsider, for example—and even then in the most abstract terms. To bring up the subject of their own mortality at any gathering of fighter pilots would be unpardonable bad taste. They will rehash the bandit's fiery demise all night from every angle. But their own death is a very private matter, rarely expressed in words.

The fighter pilot mystique is the reason behind the F-4 pilots' love-hate relationship with their weapons systems operators, the navigators who ride behind them in the cockpit. WSOs are not copilots, even though there is a vestigial control stick along with some other auxiliary flight systems in the "whizzo's" cockpit. The F-4 can be flown from the back seat, but it makes both crewmen uncomfortable. The best crews like to keep the separation of powers intact; the pilot flies the plane, the WSO operates the radar, monitors the radio, and in a fight, keeps his eyes peeled for enemy aircraft.

The fighter pilot community has always been ambivalent about the WSOs and has gone through a number of nicknames for the men who ride in the backseat, trying to come up with a term that would clearly define their role. In the early stages of the Vietnam War, the pilots were called aircraft commanders and the WSOs *were* called pilots—in fact, many whizzos were rated pilots, waiting for a chance to get into the front seat. Another favorite in Southeast Asia was "GIB," short for "guy in back." (The Navy used to call their weapons systems operators RIOs, "Radar Intercept Officers," and now has settled on NFO, "Naval Flight Officers." The Navy has always been big on having two men in the cockpit, and NFOs énjoy a clearer sense of status than their Air Force counterparts.) WSOs in F–4G Wild Weasels are called EWOs— Electronic Warfare Officers—although the term "Bears" is also popular, another holdover from Vietnam. A Luftwaffe whizzo is a *kampfbeobachter* (KBO), literally a "battle observer," perhaps, according to one fighter pilot, the best-ever definition of the WSO's role.

Informally, a WSO might be an "Ace of Gauges," "Scope Dope," " 'Gator' or "Fightergator" (derivations of "navigator"), a "Pitter" or "Prisoner of the Pit," the last two stemming from the whizzo's location—the backseat, because of its restricted vision, is known as the "pit." Whizzos have no corresponding nickname for pilots, except for the obscure term "Nosegunner," hung on some F–4E pilots by their backseaters.

Although fighter pilots express nothing but admiration and respect for their own WSOs, they are ambiguous about them as a breed. Whizzos have no place in the romance of the single combat warrior; knights in shining aircraft do not ride double when they joust. For their part, the WSOs feel they deserve all the credit they get. After all, they take the same risks and plot the intercept to get the pilot lined up for the best shot. They resent being thought of as excess baggage, but knowing the Air Force's adoration of the fighter pilot, do not make a fuss. They are resigned to life in the pit,

doomed forever to follow a respectful forty-four inches behind the pilot.

There is some evidence that the WSO is an aberration in fighter design, a human stopgap, to be replaced by microcircuitry as soon as possible. All the USAF's newest tactical aircraft are single seaters. Critics suggest the work load in the new fighters nudges the task-saturation level, that there will never be a substitute for the second pair of hands and eyes in the cockpit, but it appears the Air Force whizzo is a vanishing breed. When the last F–4 is taken out of the USAF inventory, the WSOs will be out of a job. Some might be able to get rides in the F–4G or the F–111. Or the Air Force might decide to buy the two-seat F–15E "Strike Eagle" interdictor.

But one thing is clear: As the newer fighters are being introduced, the F–4 is slowly being pushed out of the air-to-air mission and into a strictly ground-attack role. And even if the Air Force buys the F–15E, or the similar two-seat F–16 "Scamp," the WSO has a limited future in the fighter business.

The new fighters are built for the single combat warrior. The F–15, especially, is exactly the kind of aircraft fighter pilots say they would most want to go to war in. With its huge wings and mighty engines it can either out-climb, out-turn, or outrun any aircraft in the Soviet inventory. It was designed for one mission—air-to-air combat—and does it better than any aircraft in the world. The F–15 is the USAF's first dedicated air-superiority fighter since the F–86 of the Korean War. It is the final product of the Air Force's Fighter Experimental (FX) program, the result of lessons learned in Vietnam, a kind of airborne Darwinism that states the sky belongs to those most capable of surviving in it.

The motto of the FX program was "all-superiority." Although the F–15 has some ground attack capability, it was not designed for anything but air-to-air; "Not a pound for air-to-ground!" was the

team cheer of the F–15 development program led by a chorus of fighter pilots and USAF brass. Just how good a fighter is the F–15? Ask the man who doesn't fly one:

The F–15 will make an above-average pilot out of a hamburger (says an envious F–4 crewman). *You put that same hamburger in an F–4 and it* (his hamburgerness) *is going to become very apparent.*

The F–15's a lot more forgiving an airplane. You want to go up? Pull the stick up, light the engine — you've got a more than one-to-one thrust-to-weight ratio—and you're going to go up, that's all there is to it. The F–15 is so far and away the best airplane in the world you can't even call it an airplane compared to everything else.

Loaded 86th TFW F-4Es blast off from the strip at Ramstein. The older-generation Phantom remains a formidable strike aircraft.

In fact, if it wasn't for the F–16, F–15 pilots would bliss out in perpetual Sierra Hotel fighter jock Nirvana. *The F–16! Arrgh!* Eagle pilots always have a few choice words reserved for the Air Combat Fighter, the Little Hummer, the Condor, the Electric Jet, the Viper, the Fighting Falcon, or whatever they're calling the F–16 this week. It's not that the Eagle pilots think the F–16 is a dog, far from it. It is a prodigy in the strike role. But as a fighter it has certain limitations, as F–15 pilots are quick to point out.

There are too many myths surrounding the F-16. It has been said the aircraft can accelerate while climbing straight up; it cannot. It has been said the F-16's top speed is in the Mach 2 range, but its fixed inlet makes it doubtful the aircraft could achieve that under anything resembling operational conditions. (This is not a serious drawback, however. Almost every aircraft with an advertised speed of Mach 2 rarely approaches it in actual use; nor does it need to.) It has been said the F-16 cannot be over-G'd, and this is also untrue. The F-16 *can* be over-G'd in the air-to-ground configuration, its most common mission in USAFE, because the bomb racks have a G-limit less than the airframe.

However, in the air-to-air configuration with full internal fuel, the F-16 is stressed for nine Gs. The airframe could probably sustain even more stress, but the pilots can't, so the F-16 has a magic G-limiter that prevents the aircraft from pulling more Gs than the pilot can take. The F-16 is also said to have some restrictive angle-of-attack limitations and is often skittish in formation flight and landing.

This is not meant to be a gratuitous knock of the F-16, which is a highly successful aircraft, particularly in the air-to-surface role. Since the F-16 and the F-15 share the same type of engine, they have comparable acceleration, deceleration, roll, and turn performance. This makes the F-16 a ferocious close-in dogfighter. But it does not make it an air-superiority aircraft. It lacks the radar and beyond-visual-range missiles of the F-15, or even the F-4. This leads to long and heated debate about IFF (Identification Friend or Foe), rules of engagement, cheap fighters, and defense politics. We will get into *that* later.

The F-16 versus F-15 debate is a red herring, anyway, an old argument that the media, goaded by the contractors, likes to jaw about on slow news days. Like the other bogus battles of the century (F-15 versus F-14, F-14 versus F-18, even A-10 versus—believe it!—P-51), the F-15 versus F-16 debate doesn't make much sense unless the United States suddenly declares war on Belgium (a thought that has passed through the minds of many Bitburg pilots, especially when the Belgian boys from Beauvechain show up with their F-16s to challenge the Eagle jocks to a duel in the sky and then suggest the Americans behave like gentlemen and leave their radars and radar missiles at home).

But one fact has been overlooked in the smoke of the F-15 versus F-16 debate: The two aircraft work wonderfully well *together.* Because of their comparable flight performance, the F-15s and F-16s are able to maintain mutual support during the initial interception and maneuvering phases of an engagement. The F-15 acts as a sort of "mini-AWACS," using its long-range radar to vector the F-16s and engage the targets beyond visual range with its Sparrow missiles. The F-16s sneak around behind the enemy aircraft under cover from the F-15s, or wait until the F-15s charge through the hostile formation and pick off the bad guys as they try to reverse to engage the Eagles.

No matter which type of aircraft is operated, all fighter squadron operations areas look pretty much the same; the only real difference is what kind of plastic fighter will chase the plastic MiGs across the ceiling of the intelligence shop. By the entrance, there will be what looks like a hotel reception desk, and a grid behind it will display the squadron's daily operations. There will be briefing rooms, some with videotape machines, where pilots review cassettes of the day's missions. Bulletin boards will be plastered with advisories, safety notices, and snapshots of the squadron personnel at play.

And there will always be a squadron lounge, inevitably decorated in a hideous style found elsewhere only in the condos of recently divorced bachelors. There will be a stand-up bar at one end and, behind it, a refrigerator stocked with beer. Its

door will be covered with souvenir stickers from other units and notes imploring the pilots to pay up. There will be suburban Daddy chairs distributed randomly around the room, and over in a corner there will be a video game that doesn't work. (At the 525th Tactical Fighter Squadron lounge in Bitburg, the Bulldogs have a video game that doesn't work and a jukebox that does, so you know they have their priorities straight.)

The fighter pilot aesthetic runs wild at squadron headquarters. It is a curious blend of Old English lettering, fine art, country and western music, locker room humor, and stenciled graphics. The only common denominator is airplanes; fighter pilots never tire of the subject. They construct models of airplanes, they sing songs about air-

Immense for a fighter, the F-15 Eagle is larger and heavier than the typical medium bomber of World War II. It is an agile dogfighter despite this apparent handicap.

planes, they make jokes about airplanes, and they paint pictures of airplanes.

The fighter pilot school of art has produced some enthralling expressions, some of it abysmally tasteless, some surprisingly good. In the what-the-hell-is-it? category, the winner is the 22nd TFS at Bitburg, where they display, in public, a tabletop sculpture of Venus Reclining studded with styrene Sparrow missiles. The legend underneath reads, "Never Turn On A Merged Plot."

17

Most fighter pilot works of art, however, are straightforward renditions of aircraft in action and are uniformly excellent. At every squadron, it seems, there is an accomplished artist in the school of Butch Aviation Realism, the kind of illustration that used to appear on model airplane box tops before it was made less visceral by truth in advertising laws.

Unfortunately, the public rarely gets a chance to see it, as the best stuff is done in the form of murals on the squadron walls. Two notable examples: At the Detachment 1 headquarters at Sembach there is a mural depicting an A-10 in the old "sausage" camouflage swooping low over a Soviet T-62 tank. And on a briefing room wall at the 10th TFS headquarters at Hahn, there is a perfectly executed, evocative study of an F-4 rolling inverted off a kiosked skyline silhouetted against a mushroom cloud.

There will also be a personal equipment room at every fighter squadron. "PE" is like a locker room in every respect. Each pilot has his own stall where he stores his gear—helmet, oxygen mask, gloves, survival vest, G-suit, "poopy suits" and "piddle packs" for long trips over water—anything he uses when flying.

Many pilots, especially the younger tigers, have helmets custom-made for them by an outfit in California. The visor on these two-hundred-dollar crash-hats is cut a bit higher than regulation USAF-issue helmets, marginally increasing the pilot's upward visibility but drastically boosting his personal sense of fashion and invulnerability. The designer helmet business is similar to a fad that swept USAF fighter bases in Southeast Asia and manifested itself in "party" suits—flimsy jump suits, custom-made in squadron colors at the American air base in Udorn, Thailand. The younger pilots' California helmets serve the same purpose: to introduce individuality into a standardized uniform and to separate the hip from the rest, this generation from the last.

The fighter pilots' brightly colored helmets are now gradually being toned down to shades of gray and white. The aircraft themselves no longer sport the bright insignia of childhood. The new look in fighters is hot rod primer gray. The color of the F-15 almost never matches the gray of the German sky, but USAFE isn't worried. Studies have shown that up to a surprisingly close distance, any aircraft—gray, silver, or bright yellow—will appear to the pilot as a black, airplane-shaped hole in the sky. The Air Force isn't saying exactly what's in the F-15's Compass Ghost Gray paint, but its overall dull finish and the fact that the paint is lighter over areas that sustain higher temperatures in flight suggest the camouflage scheme has as much to do with projecting a low infrared signature as it does with low visibility. Model airplane buffs are not crazy about the Air Force's latest low contrast craze, but the pilots kind of like it; it's so cool and tactical.

Like their helmets, the fighter pilots' G-suits are fitted to them and are theirs to keep. The G-suit is an inflatable harness that wraps around the pilot's legs like a pair of chaps. Connected to the aircraft's pressure system and "G-meter," the G-suit automatically squeezes the pilot's lower torso during violent maneuvers to keep the blood from draining to his feet. In a nine-G turn the pilot will experience a pressure nine times the weight of gravity—in real terms this means a 225-pound pilot will feel like he weighs a ton. He will have trouble lifting his arms, his flesh will feel as if it's melting on his face and running down his chin. The G-suit helps prevent "grayout" or even blackout as the blood rushes away from his head and pools in his legs.

Right: Bitburg F-15s go at it over the Ardennes Forest. Guns are usable at this close range; air-to-air missiles are fired at greater distances.

18

There are other methods used to increase G tolerance. Pilots pulling Gs go through a ritual called the "M–1 maneuver," tensing the body and expelling air in a sort of karate grunt. This accounts for the weird soundtrack on many "gun camera" videotapes. During violent maneuvers it sounds more like an X-rated movie than a radio transmission.

In addition, the ejection seat in the F–16 is reclined thirty degrees to get the pilot's head more in line with his heart. Although the actual increase in G tolerance is debatable—studies in the centrifuge show the seat must be inclined at least forty-five degrees before any real gains in G tolerance occur—F–16 pilots say the seat does improve their high-G *performance* and doesn't leave them with a sore back. (This is not a new idea. The rudder pedals of the German Me–109 World War II fighter were placed six inches higher than the Spitfire's. The raised heel-line helped keep the pilots from blacking out during abrupt maneuvers.)

Fighter pilots also improve their G tolerance by working out. In F–16 squadrons, where pilots routinely pull nine Gs not because they have to but because they *can,* it is not uncommon to see men working out with neck exercise machines. Sore necks and stiff backs are common problems in fighter squadrons, caused by keeping track of opponents while executing wrenching turns.

A related problem is *petechiasis,* the rupture of capillaries during high-G engagements. Called "high-G measles" or "fighter hickeys," the symptoms are tingling and itching, accompanied by bruiselike skin discolorations. New pilots or vets returning to the cockpit after a long layoff are common petechiasis sufferers. F–15 pilots usually get them on their buttocks, their abdomen, or under their arms; F–16 pilots, because of the inclined seat, most commonly contract them on their legs and underarms.

Petechiasis may be annoying, but it's nothing compared to the dangers that accompany fighter pilots on even the most routine flights. There are more ways to get killed flying fighters than in practically any other human endeavor. Nowhere else does a worker encounter occupational hazards like hypoxia (pilots are not allowed to give blood), vertigo, or caisson disease ("the bends").

The aircraft itself is kept aloft by a shaky detente of unforgiving physics and capricious science; no amount of engineering or number of safety inspections can prevent something from going wrong sometime. Even if the pilot manages to eject, there is no guarantee he will land safely. There have been great improvements in ejection seats in the last generation of aircraft, but no one has solved the tricky problem of rocketing a human being cleanly out of an aircraft at six hundred knots into supercold air with unfailing success. The average person tends to think of an ejection seat as a sort of escalator to the ground, but pilots know it is an extremely dangerous business, to be undertaken only as a last resort.

The Air Force is unique among the services in that the officers take the risks. There may not be any atheists in foxholes, but it would be rare to find anyone above the rank of captain in one either. The Navy's planes are flown by officers, it is true. Yet the officers and men of the surface and subsurface task forces are, literally, in the same boat. But in the Air Force, it's the lieutenants, captains, majors, and colonels who fly and fight. There are no enlisted aircrew aboard any USAFE tactical aircraft.

This situation has led to the intertwining of the two USAF hierarchies: In order to fly you must be an officer; in order to be an officer and commander in the squadron, you must be able to fly. As an officer rises in rank, his organizational and command skills become more critical, but to lead he must gain respect and pull his own weight in the air. The Air Force's fascination with the fighter pilot isn't the relationship of sycophant to star; it is more the concern of a father who knows from experience

Seymour-Johnson F-4 jocks in an informal debrief after trans-Atlantic flight to their co-location base at Ramstein.

how tough life can be and wants only the best for his son.

Everybody flies in the fighter wings. The wing commander, his deputies and staff officers—dubbed "wing weenies" by the pilots—all have to prove themselves in the air. They are what is known as Rated Position Indicator Codes, called "Rippys," pilots who are not attached to a squadron like the regular line jocks but usually fly with a particular squadron in order to keep current. There are about seven Rippys for each of the wing's three squadrons, known by numbers denoting their rank—a "Rippy 6," for example, is a flying colonel, an awesome thing to behold.

At the top of the wing command structure is the wing commander. He is the boss, usually a full colonel, sometimes even a general. He is responsible for everything, and everyone is responsible to him.

To help him keep track of the countless oper-ational details of running the unit, the wing commander delegates authority to his subordinates. The wing's vice-commander is in charge during the CO's absence. The CV is often responsible for the wing's local readiness exercises in his capacity as the wing inspector. Another senior officer, the base commander, supervises support facilities—housekeeping chores such as civil engineering, security police, and personnel. During a reorganization of the wing structure in the 1970s, the base commander was given a hand with his heavy work load by the creation of a new position. The deputy commander for resources assumed control of some of the operations that were formerly the

21

jurisdiction of the base commander: supply, finance, and the transportation squadron, for example.

From the pilot's point of view, the key man at the wing level is the deputy commander for operations (DO). The DO is in charge of the wing's flying operations. His nearest Navy equivalent, to give an example of his importance, is the ship's executive officer. The three squadron commanders "work for" the DO.

The DO controls the wing's important operational sections: The command post is the command and control hub of the wing. The intelligence unit processes information from a higher level and distributes it to the squadrons. The plans shop draws up most of the operational plans the wing must have, usually outgrowths of some USAF, USAFE, or NATO plan. The standardization-evaluation group is very important to pilots; it administers the check-rides and evaluates the

pilots' proficiency. The weapons and tactics shop keeps the squadrons informed about the capabilities, use, and limitations of the wing's weapons and has a lot of input into training.

Most of these functions are mirrored in the squadron structure. The squadron commander even has his own version of the DO in the form of the squadron ops officer.

Another key officer at the wing level has no squadron equivalent. He is the Deputy Com-

Left: F-15s approach Bitburg at conclusion of "1 v. 1" air-to-air session.

Above: Visual contact is the toughest but most crucial element of aerial combat.

mander for Maintenance (DCM). The DCM's difficult job is keeping the wing's nervous, expensive, and delicate aircraft ready to fly. This is not the same as flying them, however, and whenever the DCM is forced to pull a plane off the line for preventive maintenance, routine inspections, or just to fix it, he is apt to find himself toe-to-toe with the DO, whose business *is* flying and who is in no mood to listen to sad but true stories about spares shortages and lack of maintenance personnel. This built-in adversary relationship often leads to bad blood and bitter feelings and is not helped by the fact that, in USAFE, the DCMs are pilots but not Rippys and do not fly. Inevitably, in the best wings the DO and the DCM have come to a mutual understanding, usually negotiated by the wing commander.

24

Ground crews prepare an F-15 of the 22nd TFS, Bitburg, for a mission.

"That's one thing that will get a wing in trouble, if the DO and the DCM can't agree and are at each other's throats, because they've got to work together," says a USAFE wing commander. "They're like two people handcuffed together in a rowboat —they'll never get anywhere unless they decide to row in the same direction."

Like the DO, the DCM exercises his authority through a number of specialized units: The programs and mobility group includes training, administration, and deployment support. Maintenance control coordinates the daily maintenance operations and keeps track of the status of the wing's aircraft from a centralized command bunker. The DCM's staff of specialists and inspectors check and evaluate the work of the crews, but the actual maintenance is performed by three maintenance squadrons.

The most visible of these is the aircraft generation squadron (AGS), which is divided into three line branches called aircraft maintenance units. The AMUs are designated by the same number as the squadron they support. Each AMU consists of a specialist flight, a weapons flight, and two APG (aircraft personnel group) flights, more often called "crew chiefs." In the past, crew chiefs were usually three-stripers, but now it is not uncommon to see airmen—two- or even one-stripers—serving in that capacity.

This is not as alarming as it sounds. The airmen do a good job, and although crew chiefs must have a lot of dedication and common sense it is not a position that requires an extensive amount of training. Modern aircraft are extremely complex, but paradoxically, they are easier to maintain on the flight line than aircraft of an earlier generation.

This is because maintainability has been built into the latest aircraft, whose more complex functions have been compartmentalized into Line Replaceable Units. These LRUs are often referred to as "black boxes"; they are sophisticated avionics and electronics packages that slide in and out of the aircraft.

LRUs have their good and bad points. On the plus side, they allow easier and quicker flight line maintenance by less-trained personnel. The black boxes can be switched around from aircraft to aircraft with little trouble. Broken LRUs can be pulled from the aircraft and fixed on a workbench using specialized testing equipment. It is no longer necessary to taxi the whole aircraft to a hangar to work on its electronic systems.

On the other hand, a broken black box is still broken. And even though the older generation of aircraft were more difficult to work on—changing the battery or fixing the radio in an F-4 is a particularly nightmarish experience for maintenance crews—they could sometimes be fixed on the flight line by a little tweaking. But because of their solid-state nature, no amount of tweaking will fix a broken black box. It must be taken to a special shop with the right kind of diagnostic equipment. This often leads to "hidden" maintenance time. The black boxes may be swapped from aircraft to aircraft, but it's like a game of musical chairs: Sooner or later there's going to be one aircraft, or two, or eight, that are not fully mission capable (FMC) because of LRU problems. In the early days of the F-15 deployment, cannibalization of parts was a big problem. But since the spares pipeline began to flow, the FMC rates have gone way up.

FMC rates are often misunderstood by the press and public. If an aircraft is not fully mission capable, that doesn't mean it's completely useless, that it can't fly or fight. There may be some systems that aren't functioning, or not functioning the way they should, but in a wartime situation all such restrictions would be thrown out and the aircraft would go to battle anyway, if needed.

The F-15's engine is a perfect example of this. One F-100 engine costs about two million dollars and they come in pairs. The Air Force is very careful with the engines, and rightly so. At the slightest hint of trouble they will ground the aircraft, pull the engines out (maintenance crews can change an F-15 engine in an hour and a half), and examine them very, very closely. This sort of caution initially led to low FMC rates for the F-15, which were pointed out in the press as indications that the Eagle was a very nervous bird indeed.

The press likes to glob on to something that they think will have high interest and some impact, and when you're talking about expensive airplanes, that has interest and impact (says a USAFE wing commander). *If expensive airplanes are not performing well, then they feel there's a service being done to point that out.*

The F-100 engine in the F-15 took an awful lot of flak, and is still taking some, but not near as much. But it's right on the leading edge of engine technology and you almost have to expect you're going to have some problems. The Air Force made a conscious decision to put the airplane in the inventory at the expense of some element of support because we needed to have the F-15s operational. And we're paying that price and we're catching up now.

His DCM agrees:

The F-15 has always had a reliable engine. Even when we had core problems and we had holes, if we went to war we'd go to different criteria—we'd stuff the holes and fly the engines. The only reason we pulled them out of service was to protect them, to prevent damage to the engines, to repair them before they failed. But if we had had to use them to generate, I would have used them. They were flyable engines, operational engines.

The DCM juggles men and spares to keep the aircraft flying. If he had an endless supply of black boxes and spare engines he could keep them flying around the clock. But life is never that simple. The LRUs are too expensive to keep lying around in boxes. They must be repaired on the base.

This is done by the Component Repair Squadron (CRS), which also maintains the engines and moni-

tors engineering standards for the wing. It's the most intricate and labor-intensive engineering work performed at the wing level. Third generation aircraft are characterized by capability and its shadow, complexity. Training someone to fix them is difficult. Keeping the trained personnel is getting to be impossible, and when you hear people talk about the lack of qualified enlisted maintenance crewmen in today's USAF, they're talking about the CRS. The Air Force used to lose these people at a hemorrhaging rate to private companies who could double their pay and cut their work load in half. The loss rate has slowed down a lot now as the civilian economy has weakened, but getting, training, and keeping experienced maintenance personnel is one of the Air Force's biggest problems.

The DCM's third squadron is the Equipment Maintenance Squadron (EMS). Besides handling the wing's missiles and munitions, this unit also performs the countless scheduled aircraft inspections. They replace equipment that has time-change requirements and do the deeper maintenance: lubricating the aircraft and inspecting the airframe for cracks. The EMS also maintains the wing's aerospace ground equipment—the powered and nonpowered generators, test stations, anything the maintenance crews use in their work.

F-15 units average about five and a half direct man-hours to "turn" an aircraft—recover it, get it ready to go again, and launch it. On a mission it can be done in less than an hour and a half, but this means pushing more people into the system.

There are five maintenance crew members involved in a turnaround: The crew chief will supervise the "stuffing"—pushing the aircraft back in the hangar with cables. Another crew chief, really an assistant, will check over the aircraft from the outside. A three-man load crew will reload the aircraft with missiles and gun rounds. A fuel truck driver will fill the plane's tanks. It costs about five thousand dollars to fill up an F-15. They use JP-4

fuel, but are cross-matched for Jet A-1, the type of fuel used by most commercial airliners. This is the closest thing to a common NATO aircraft fuel there is—the British have converted completely to Jet A-1—and the ability to use different types of fuel would become vitally important in a wartime situation.

The "hangars" are not hangars in the usual sense. They are "TAB Vs," Theater Air Base Vulnerability Shelters, a type of hardened aircraft shelter peculiar to USAFE. Construction began in Germany in the late 1960s after Department of Defense studies concluded that parked aircraft were particularly vulnerable to airfield attacks with conventional weapons. The TAB Vs are now standard throughout most USAFE bases in Germany. Made of steel and surrounded by a quonset-type roof of concrete two feet thick, the shelter's inner lining of corrugated steel prevents fragments of concrete from spalling the interior during an attack.

The TAB Vs are 48 feet wide, 120 feet long, and 24 feet high. At the back there is a port to funnel jet engine exhaust out of the shelter; at the front there are heavy steel doors that can be opened by one man. Only one aircraft can fit into a shelter, and there is usually a shelter for each aircraft.

Many continental USAFE bases were designed by the French and built by the Germans. The French architecture is still evident at many bases in the form of the "French TAB V." This is not a real TAB V in the strict sense, just a concrete bunker, a sort of garage open at both ends and surrounded by earth. They do not offer nearly the protection of the new TAB Vs, and are now used more for storing equipment than parking aircraft.

Another type of construction exclusive to USAFE is the new hardened ops center. These

Right: Hardened TAB-V hangars provide protection for Bitburg F-15s. At most USAFE bases each bird has its own TAB-V.

are the military equivalent of the civilian fallout shelters, built so the squadron can continue operations even if the base is hit by a chemical warfare attack. On the outside, the hardened ops center is a gray concrete slab. On the inside there is space for all the functions the squadron needs to carry on life as usual—for a while anyway—even though the base outside may be clouded in a fog of Sarin gas. The pilots get in and out of the shelter through a rat's maze of decontamination stations.

Last-minute electronics check at Bitburg end-of-runway inspection area. Latest-generation electronics are mounted in modular "black boxes" that can be pulled and replaced in minutes.

They throw their exposed flight suits into an incinerator and walk around the squadron in a sort of paper pajama outfit. As the hardened ops centers become more common in USAFE the squadrons will begin to make themselves at home in the shel-

ters and will transfer many of the day-to-day functions they now carry on in their frame buildings to the new "command condos."

Tactical fighter squadrons have eighteen to twenty-four aircraft and a shade more than that many pilots. The squadron is divided into four flights, designated by the first four letters of the alphabet. A new pilot coming into the squadron will be assigned to one of the flights, where he will be paired with an experienced pilot, his new wing-

Airmen drill in chemical gear while performing F-15 maintenance at Bitburg. Periodic alerts require wearing of clumsy suits for full day.

man. The new jock will go through an exhaustive indoctrination program before he will be declared "MR," mission ready. His training syllabus consists of a seemingly endless series of check-rides and evaluations supervised by the squadron's training shop in accordance with USAFE readiness guidelines that are very specific as to how much of what kind of training a particular pilot must have to be mission ready.

But a great deal of the new pilot's introduction to USAFE will not be written down. In fact, the most important element of his new life in the air-to-air arena will never be found in any book; it is the contract he will work out with his new wingman.

The contract. There's a great buzz word for you. Mention air combat to a standard military aviation buff and he'll start spouting off about corner velocity, wing loading, and a bunch of other hardware-related nonsense that will convince you he has no idea of what's really going on. But to a pilot, air combat means the contract. It is the secret word. Nothing more need be said.

Basically, the contract is a verbal agreement between two people, usually a pilot and his wingman, but also between a pilot and his whizzo. It covers operational procedures, plans for attack and defense, code words—anything the pilots use when flying and especially when fighting, will be worked out in great detail between the two men on the ground and in the air.

The contract is never written down, but it is more binding than anything the pilot will ever sign. It may be changed only by mutual consent. The penalty for not fulfilling the contract is to be branded a Whiskey Delta, with all the personal and professional demerits that implies. In wartime, the consequences of a broken contract are even more severe—the death of one, or both, pilots.

The contract is not a concept limited to fighter pilots. The new jock will have had contracts since his first days of training, but whereas those contracts dealt with rather simple contingencies— what to do if the instructor pilot was incapacitated by a bird strike, for example—the tactical fighter contract is a more serious matter, going into much greater detail. Everything has to be worked out and understood before the fight. There won't be

time to jabber about it on the radio—at 600 knots in a turning, confused dogfight, no pilot wants to have to ask his wingman where he is and what he's doing. He wants to *know,* and with a well thought out contract followed to the letter, he will.

There have been contracts as long as there have been wingmen, but there hasn't always been a name for it. The recent interest in contracts is due to the USAF's switch in emphasis from a four-ship to a two-ship formation.

In Vietnam, the formation the Air Force used most often was the "Fluid Four": two pairs— elements—of aircraft, separated by about 2,000 feet horizontally, 3,000 to 4,000 feet vertically, and 5,000 to 8,000 feet laterally. The formation resembled a box with the two elements on opposite corners.

The wingmen flew a "welded wing" slightly behind and about 1,000 feet beside their element leader. In combat they would try to stay on the inside of the turns as close to the leader as possible. The idea of the Fluid Four was to give the wingman, who was generally the less-experienced pilot of the element, a chance to taste combat under the guidance of a veteran leader. In practice the formation succeeded in getting a lot of wingmen killed as the leader would take off after targets and glory, leaving the wingman behind to fend for himself. As any USAFE pilot will tell you, it's the ones left behind that are shot down. The Fluid Four also presented the enemy with not one, but two overlapping "lethal cones"—areas of vulnerability projecting from the rear of the aircraft—without a corresponding increase in the element's offensive potential.

In the later stages of the war, the Navy began using a two-ship fighter formation. The "Loose Deuce" was basically the same arrangement as the Fluid Four, but where the Air Force used a pair of aircraft in each element, the Navy essentially used just one. This maximized the advantages of the Fluid Four and minimized its disadvantages. It

Ramstein F-4E approaches tanker near gunnery range at Zaragosa, Spain.

Loose Deuce, known as the "Fluid Two." It is roughly a line-abreast formation, with wide lateral and altitudinal separation. The Air Force is also experimenting with the concept of "Linked Pairs," several Fluid Twos fighting independently but able to call on other Fluid Twos nearby for support.

The USAF is very close-mouthed about specifics of the tactical formations they fly. The positioning of the aircraft in a Fluid Two will depend on the mission as well as the expected threat. Aircraft also routinely switch their relative positions in flight; coupled with the wide separation, this shell game helps insure that even if an enemy were to spot one aircraft in the formation, he wouldn't know exactly where to look to spot the other one. For the record, the two Navy F-14s that shot down the Libyan fighters over the Gulf of Sidra in 1981 were flying a Loose Deuce formation, line-abreast and two miles apart, separated by about 4,000 feet in altitude.

"The Navy is big on a two-ship employment concept and that's what I've been trying to drive toward here in the squadron," says a Hahn squadron commander who flew the Loose Deuce on an exchange tour with the Navy.

The four-ship is a little unwieldy, I think. But with the two-ship you can always mate those two crews together; every time they're on the schedule it's the same two guys. That way there are a lot of things that are standard between them that they don't have to cover every time they fly (the contract). *With the call signs it simplifies everything.*

A call sign is a code word used to identify a flight of aircraft. The individual aircraft are designated by number, so if the flight's call sign were "SPAD" (a popular name), then the flight leader would be "SPAD 01," his wingman "SPAD 02," and so on.

There are no deep, underlying meanings to the call signs. They don't signify anything in particular; just about any easily understandable one- or two-syllable word will do. Favorite themes for call signs in Southeast Asia were automobiles (BUICK,

had greater appeal to the wingmen; since there were more opportunities for changes of tactical lead in a two-ship formation, the wingman became more of a partner and less of a target. No longer did he just get shot at. In the Loose Deuce he had a chance to shoot back.

The Air Force has adopted the two-ship formation, informally if not officially. Some strike aircraft still travel in a variation of the four-ship, and "heavies" like tankers and high-altitude B–52s fly in "cells" of three aircraft, but most fighter squadrons have gone to the USAF's version of the

CHEVY, RAMBLER), cities (TAMPA, OAKLAND, VEGAS), weapons (HARPOON, PISTOL, CROSSBOW), animals (BISON, PANDA, OTTER), sea creatures (OYSTER, CRAB, LEECH), and birds (EAGLE, FALCON, LARK).

The call signs are changed frequently to confuse enemy units monitoring friendly radio transmissions. In Vietnam the call signs were changed so often pilots sometimes resorted to writing the operative call signs on their canopies to remind themselves of who they were on that particular day. Even so, in the heat of battle many fighter pilots *did* forget the call signs, and would resort to warning a comrade of impending disaster in plain, nonoperational English, addressing the endangered pilot by his first name.

RF-4C recon pilot breaks left to begin rapid descent for photo run. Photo pass will be made at minimum altitude, maximum speed.

Since there were often up to a hundred aircraft on the same strike package frequency there were bound to be pilots with the same first names on the same net. This inevitably led to some confusion. The worst possible case would be to have a wingman named "Sam," as in "SAM break right!" The offending pilot would then be treated to the stirring sight of all one hundred planes executing a gut-wrenching 90-right in unison and, upon landing, a stern lecture on radio discipline by the squadron CO.

34

The call signs are a sore spot between USAFE pilots and their higher-ups. Back when the two-ship formation was beginning to gain acceptance, there was a move by the pilots to use their nicknames as call signs instead of having call signs arbitrarily issued to them on different flights. The system of "tactical call signs" had several advantages. The names would automatically denote the flight leader's identity; the other ship in the formation would have the same call sign (the leader's nickname) but would be identified by a different number to distinguish between the two aircraft on GCI (ground control intercept) transmissions. In intraformation calls, however, both planes would be known simply by the leader's nickname, as in a two-ship they could only be talking to one another.

F-4E driver awaits last-minute checks at Ramstein. Crewmen walk around aircraft, seeking fluid leaks, open doors, unusual sounds.

The nicknames are short and graphic, easily remembered in the unlikely event that the pilots didn't know them already. And no two nicknames are alike: If two pilots show up at the base with the same nickname, the junior officer is graciously required to change his to avoid confusion. Otherwise there would be as many "Killers" at Bitburg as there are "MacGregors" in Glasgow.

The tactical call signs seemed like a good idea, and like most good ideas thought up by the rank and file it soon ran into some difficulty. A Bitburg pilot explains why:

These tactical call signs are becoming somewhat out of vogue right now because it was perceived in a number of aircraft accidents that these names somehow intimated a lack of flight discipline—calling people "Rowdy" and "Bozo" and all the neat names fighter pilots tend to come up with —when in fact they had a very real purpose.

So, for a while in the tactical air forces they were prohibited. Now we're back to using call signs and numbers again. Re-inventing the wheel is a little game we play from time to time.

Nicknames are standard issue in the fighter pilot fraternity. Everybody has one, usually hung on him early in his career by an instructor pilot or another guy in the unit. Some are the result of an unfortunate episode a pilot would rather forget but is cursed by his very nickname to live with for the rest of his tactical life. Some of the nicknames, like "Tex," "Mad Dog," and "Zip Gun," are rather ordinary in a fighter pilot sort of way. But others— "Shoes," "Splash," and "Hooter," for instance— are stories waiting to be told.

The nicknames are a source of pride, and before the tactical call signs were banned, pilots used to sport them on their uniform name-tags in place of their regular names. The nickname tags still make an occasional appearance at the O-Club bar on Friday nights, when USAFE pilots are feeling particularly rebellious.

As denigrating as some of the nicknames are, to be without one is even worse. There is a story told at Hahn of the Man Without a Nickname.

Now, this man had a perfectly good given name, but it was one of those names like Robin or Francis that is given to both men and women; to save him even further embarrassment we'll call him Lynn. Lynn was tired of his sexually ambiguous name, tired of being taken for a female in correspondence, and joined the Air Force, some squadron cynics say, just to trade in his hated Christian name for a new, more macho *nom de guerre.* And his fellow pilots, first out of oversight and then out of sheer perversity, refused to give him one.

Lynn tried everything to get a nickname. He hinted. He assumed names that didn't stick. At one point, when the squadron was deployed in Spain, he went out and bought a bunch of bullfighting equipment, desperately hoping his buddies would pick up on it and call him Swords or Zorro—anything but Lynn. But they never did, and after a while even Lynn got the joke and now carries his indelible wimpy name with pride, like a real fighter pilot nickname with a story behind it and everything.

A pilot usually learns of his mission the day before, when the next day's flying operations are posted on the grid. The "shell" is a list of takeoff times, call signs, and the type of mission. Other information will be posted later.

The pilots who will take part in the mission attend a flight briefing about two hours prior to takeoff. The briefing lasts from forty-five minutes to an hour. Any of the pilots can plan the mission, but it is the responsibility of the flight leader—usually the pilot flying the first aircraft but not always the senior officer of the flight—to see that the mission is correctly planned. It is not unusual to have different "players" each plan a part of a complicated mission. It often takes more time to plan the mission than to fly it.

The flight leader fills out a "lineup" card repeating the information on the shell, as well as new information, such as the names of the pilots and the numbers and locations of the aircraft that will be flown on the mission. The briefing goes into great detail: how the flight will check in on the radio; how they will start engines, taxi, and take off; the NOTAMs (Notices to Airmen) that affect various bases; the weather and the weather alternatives; all the way down to landing and recovery.

The flight leader will then discuss what type of training mission it is. Each mission is carefully

planned with specific training objectives in mind. The flight leader will brief on the type of ordnance that will be employed, who the simulated "bad guys" will be, and what constitutes a "kill."

The planes will not carry live ordnance on a training mission, of course. But the HUD (Head Up Display) will give the pilots very precise feedback on their gunsights, so there's no need to carry live rounds for Vulcan cannon. And the planes will carry plugs for the AIM–7 radar missiles that provide information to the HUD and the armament control set on the left side of the console. They also carry one heat-seeking training missile, a captive AIM–9P or AIM–9L with a live guidance and control unit, but no motor or warhead. This makes for a realistic training exercise: "You get all the indications that you would when you actually fire

Pilot's-eye view of F-15's Head-Up Display. HUD projects basic flight, navigation, and weapons information in pilot's line of forward vision.

the missiles, except when you hit the button nothing comes off the airplane," says a Bitburg fighter pilot.

The trouble is the other guy has difficulty knowing when he's shot, especially since he doesn't want to believe it. Kill removal and re-entry are the stickiest problems of any training mission. The two or three engagements the flight manages to squeeze in on a typical mission are constantly marred by confusion, as "dead" pilots continue to live or come back to life too quickly.

F-15s departing Bitburg on training flight; Zulu Alert shack is below nose of lead aircraft. Zulu planes roll directly from firehouselike hangars onto runway for take-off.

As the pilots come out of the briefing room they will check the board to see if there are any changes. Then they'll suit up in the Personal Equipment room and head out to the aircraft, usually about fifty minutes prior to takeoff. Sometimes they'll walk, but if the weather is as bad as usual, or if their aircraft is parked at a TAB V way out on the perimeter they'll hitch a ride in one of the ubiquitous dark green Volkswagen vans that troll USAFE bases like New York taxicabs.

Although the squadrons have specific planes assigned to them, the pilots do not. A pilot may have his name stenciled on an aircraft, but the one he flies on any particular mission depends purely upon chance; the maintenance crews generate the planes, and he takes the next in line.

Some pilots may not even have their names on an aircraft. Fighter jocks have been known to pass up this opportunity for immortality if it means having their names plastered on the side of a "tub," the two-seat trainer version of the F-15. Most squadrons have a couple of tubs assigned to them for training and check-rides. The two-seat F-15Ds are identical to the single seat F-15Cs in terms of weapons capability and flight characteristics. But style counts, and young tigers will often decide that having their name on a squadron tub is *not* better than nothing and prefer to wait for another "regular" fighter with a vacant canopy rail.

Once the pilots locate their aircraft in the TAB Vs they "preflight" them, checking the planes against maintenance records, looking for outstanding "write-ups" that would affect the mission. The crew has already done this, but the pilots are "buying" the aircraft administratively, as well as in a very real sense. Then they climb into the cockpit and set up their personal gear, stowing maps and charts where they'll be handy but out of the way.

Although modern combat aircraft are much more complex and capable than their predecessors, they are, paradoxically, easier to fly from a stick-and-rudder point of view. This is because many of the routine mechanical and "housekeeping" chores, such as navigation, communication, and computation of weapons parameters and release points have been greatly reduced or taken over completely by on-board computers.

Most of the latest generation of Western combat aircraft have a HUD, or Head Up Display. The HUD is a sheet of glass perched above the forward instrument panel at a forty-five degree angle. A projection system displays computer-generated navigational and weapons information on the HUD, so the pilot can keep his eyes "out of the cockpit" and still keep a constant reading of such vital information as heading, altitude, airspeed, angle of attack, or any of the dozens of parameters he can dial up from the cockpit.

Ergonomics, the science of designing machinery for safety and comfort, is present throughout the rest of the cockpit. The USAF has a design philosophy called HOTAS, for Hands on Throttle and Stick, which means a pilot's hands should never have to leave his throttle or his stick, and his eyes should never have to go back into the cockpit in a fight. So everything the pilot needs in a dogfight is at his fingertips; all the information he needs is on the HUD. After it was discovered that situating the radio panel down in the cockpit interior contributed to a number of aircraft accidents, especially those occurring right after takeoff, when pilots were forced to go "heads down" to change frequencies, the frequency selector on most modern aircraft is placed high and forward, right underneath the HUD. The switches and dials inside the cockpit are all different shapes, so the pilot can tell, by feel if necessary, which switch is which.

The flight controls are also designed with the pilot in mind. The rudder is fed in automatically over most of the aircraft's flight envelope, so pilots can always make a coordinated turn. There is also automatic trim, which is a great boon to ex-Phantom jocks, because it means they can now wear flight gloves much longer without wearing out the thumbs punching the trim-tabs, as they did flying the F-4.

Not all the cockpit improvements were welcomed with open arms by the pilots. The first F-16s had an isometric stick that was located on the right side of the cockpit, rather than between the pilot's legs. It took a little getting used to, but it was okay. It also commanded Gs, which was a little strange, but still okay. But the stick didn't *move!* It responded to pressure, not movement, and that was *not* okay. As a pilot at Hahn puts it:

Fighter pilots are pretty basic people. They like to know when you pull on the pole something happens. In an F-4, when you hit a stop that's all you've got, that's all the authority that thing's going to give you. In the new generation aircraft, you're commanding Gs, for instance, and pitch, and no matter what your airspeed, it's going to try to give you that amount of G. If you don't know what the electrons are doing, I think there's a little uneasiness there.

After complaints from pilots (some of whom suffered strained muscles from trying *not* to slam the stick around) General Dynamics installed a stick that reassured the pilots with a small amount of movement.

But although modern aircraft are easier to fly, it doesn't mean flying them in combat is a piece of cake. As the flight controls have become simpler, the missions have become more complex, so today's pilots, with all their sophisticated computers and helpful cockpit ergonomics, still fly close to the saturation point.

"Don't fool yourself with these incredibly automated systems," says another pilot at Hahn.

When we put one man in an F-16 and ask him to perform all the roles that two men in an F-4 are performing, that's a lot to handle. Even switch changes become important when you're doing 600 miles an hour and you've got somebody shooting at you from the ground and somebody bouncing you from above. You've got to think fast.

An F-15 pilot agrees: "Anybody can fly the Eagle, given that he has a reasonably good set of hands. But employing it—that's a different story."

About thirty minutes prior to takeoff the flight leader will request clearance for engine start. In an F-4 the engines are started by a ground power unit, the DASH-60, a small jet engine that provides electrical power and compressed air to start the turbines. In an F-15 the pilot pulls a handle on the lower right side of the instrument panel to engage the jet fuel starter, a mechanical control that fires an accumulator bottle that in turn starts a third jet engine that sits between and below the two main engines in the Eagle. There is no battery on the F-15. The little engine provides electrical, intercom, and some hydraulic power to the aircraft. After some preliminary checks, the pilot starts the main engines off the auxiliary engine just as an automobile engine is engaged by a clutch. As soon as the main engines are started, the auxiliary engine is shut down.

After engine start, F-15 pilots will usually close the canopy. F-4 aircrew, who do not enjoy such an excellent climate control system, often leave their canopies open until the very last minute, especially in hot weather. The pilots will then run through a series of checks with the crew chiefs: cycling the flaps and the speedbrakes, checking in with the crew chiefs over the intercom to make sure the flight controls are working properly. They will also check the electronic systems using "BIT" checks—built-in test equipment on the aircraft.

At this point, if the aircraft is equipped with an Inertial Navigation System, the aircrew will align the INS, a device that looks like a pocket calculator mounted on the instrument panel. The pilot punches in his present latitude and longitude as well as other locations—the INS in an F-15 is capable of "remembering" a dozen or so locations, so on a routine training mission the pilot might punch in the boundaries of the TRA, the temporary reserved airspace the flight will be fighting in. On cross-country missions, the pilot might enter each turning point in the air route structure, as well as various geographic points, to use as a backup in case the TACAN system fails. (TACAN measures the distance and bearing between a ground point and the airplane.) The INS automatically gives a heading and distance to any selected point, and this information can be displayed on the pilot's HUD.

Although the F-15 is an all-weather aircraft and the pilots are instrument rated, in peacetime they are often grounded because of national restrictions and safety reasons. The plane is capable of being flown down to, perhaps, a 100-foot ceiling and a quarter of a mile visibility, but in the interest of safety even the most experienced F-15 jocks will rarely take off without at least a 300-foot ceiling and a mile visibility.

Most squadrons put their own restrictions on pilots. New jocks are usually restricted to an 800-foot ceiling and two miles visibility and work down from there. USAFE pilots probably do more instrument flying than most pilots in the Air Force, simply because the weather in central Europe is so execrable so often. (By the main gate at Spangdahlem, there is a neon sign that informs motorists of driving conditions. It has four modes: Wet, Slick, Fog, and Icy.) During the long German winter it is rare to have a ceiling higher than 500 feet. Bitburg pilots try to work in at least one instrument approach on every training mission and pay very close attention when the weather alternates are briefed, especially in the winter.

About ten minutes after engine starts the flight will check in again on the squadron common frequency. The squadron "freak," as it is called, would be changed constantly in a wartime situation, but during peacetime it is kept fairly constant, a popular squadron freak being "balls"—double zeroes, called "double nuts" in the Navy. The flight leader will check in the rest of the flight, and if they're set to go they will answer with "two," "three," and "four."

The flight leader will then switch to the ground control frequency (most often channel 10) and request permission to taxi, about twenty minutes prior to takeoff. The planes will taxi to an area just off the runway for an end-of-runway inspection. A "quick-check" maintenance crew will look over the aircraft for leaks, airframe damage, anything that might have gone wrong since the airplanes were warmed up and taxied out. While the "last chance" crew is inspecting the aircraft the pilots must keep their hands out of the cockpit and in plain sight so they don't accidentally throw a switch and do something to injure the crew chief under the plane.

The flight will now pull onto the runway. The flight leader switches radio frequencies once again, this time to the tower freak, usually channel 11 for USAFE bases and channel 2 for most other NATO towers. In clear weather the flight will take off in formation. In foul weather they might take off one by one, in a radar trail departure; each aircraft will have a radar lock-on to the aircraft in front, and will take off singly, twenty seconds apart.

The F-15 doesn't usually use afterburner in takeoff, and rotates at a little over 1,000 feet under most conditions. It lands in less than 3,000 feet with no drag-chute (newer aircraft like the F-15 and F-16 use a technique called aerobraking, keeping the nose up and letting wind resistance slow the aircraft down in a fighter pilot's version of a hot rod "wheelie"). The F-4, on the other hand, requires an uncomfortably long takeoff roll, even in blazing afterburner, and comes in like a screaming brick, drag-chute flaring, until it finally rolls to a stop.

The aircraft head for the Temporary Reserved Airspace and split up. The opponents will operate on separate radio frequencies, but under positive GCI (Ground Control Intercept) for safety reasons. The good guys and today's bad guys head for their respective corners of the TRA; the bell rings, the fight is on.

Although fighter aircraft and their weapons have changed a great deal since the days of the Sopwith Camel and the Lewis gun, the principles of air combat have remained surprisingly consistent. Air combat, then and now, is a sort of aerial kung fu, a blend of the physical and mental, where the opponent's energy is used against him, and where timing, strategy, and awareness count more than numbers or brute strength.

Perhaps the greatest physical attribute a pilot can have is a good pair of eyes. Although this may seem an anomaly in an era of sophisticated radar systems, there is no substitute for good vision. Many rules of engagement call for visual identification of a target before attacking, especially in the potentially confused wartime environment of central Europe, where planes of every type and nationality would be all over the sky.

Often just good eyesight is not enough. Pilots have to be trained to see—that is, they have to know what to look for and where to look for it. A MiG at three miles is smaller than a drop of water on the canopy. In almost every contract, the pilots

End-of-day Happy Hour in 525th TFS "Bulldogs" rec room. Wing DO (weird helmet, center) is about to attempt his famous breathing-fire-with-lighter-fluid trick.

split the sky into sections, each flight member being responsible for scanning his sector. Even then, F–15 pilots, who are used to sparring with other big Eagles, are routinely trounced in their first few missions against the Aggressors, because they are not accustomed to the F–5's small size.

Many F–15 pilots at Bitburg mount their own telescopic rifle scope beside the HUD. They acquire the bogies on radar and point the scope in the direction of the blip to try to get a VID, a visual identification. Some F–4s carry TISEO (Target Identification System, Electro-Optical), a stabilized video camera with a powerful zoom lens mounted on the port wing. The TISEOs are used mainly for Maverick missile delivery now, but they come in

handy during an intercept mission under visual rules of engagement.

Good vision is the key to situational awareness, the mental picture of the air battle: where the enemy is; where the friendly aircraft are; all the different speeds, angles, and altitudes of the three-dimensional aerial battlefield. Situational awareness is so important that most contracts stipulate that as soon as it is lost the flight will separate until they can get the scene sorted out clearly again.

"Unofficially, not out of a manual, you want to stay completely defensive in your formation and yet maneuverable, which is probably a line-abreast because anyone left behind is going to get shot," says a Bitburg fighter pilot.

You want to go as fast as you can go, with as much situational awareness as you can get, and attack whoever you can attack.

I've heard a philosophy: From zero to forty-five seconds, the F–15, at this time, rules any air-to-air combat engagement there is—it can kill anybody in forty-five seconds. From forty-five to sixty seconds, it's anybody's ballgame. And after sixty seconds, after the first minute, you're at a loss, because you've got so many different things going on in your aircraft.

A minute may sound like a short time, but it is an eternity in modern air combat. Current fighter tactics resemble a cavalry charge, or a joust—a rapid thrust through the enemy formation, taking whatever shots are available, separating, and regrouping on the other side. To stay in the "furball"—a confused dogfight full of swarming airplanes, friendly and unfriendly—is to risk the loss of situational awareness. Above all, F–15 pilots do not want to be drawn into a slow-speed "knife fight."

"A knife fight is where you've decided that no matter what happens you're going to slow down and kill or be killed, so now your fangs are out and you're so involved fighting this guy that somebody else can easily come in and shoot you," says an Eagle jock.

Tactically it's not a good idea. For a fighter like us, the slower you are, the less maneuverable you are, and you begin to fight their game. But sometimes a guy will decide that's what he's going to do to you and he won't let you go and you have to stay, and stay, and stay, and finally one of you dies or his buddy comes in and shoots you off.

It's not that the F–15 is a poor dogfighter; it's probably the best fighter in the world today. But in any wartime situation they would be vastly out-numbered, and in a furball numbers count for a great deal. To be drawn into a knife fight would be to negate the best features of the F–15 and fight in an arena where the enemy aircraft performs best.

This is where mutual support comes in. Sometimes a pilot must accept a dogfight or be killed trying to get away. It is the wingman's duty to protect the other pilot until he can destroy his adversary or separate.

The wingman must search his partner's rear quadrant for attackers, "check and clear six." Fighter pilots still refer to directions around their aircraft as if they were surrounded by a giant, horizontal clock pointing at high noon. By far, the most vulnerable hour is six o'clock, the area directly to the rear. It is the hardest to scan and the aircraft's most vulnerable area. The "cone of vulnerability," another imaginary fighter pilot device, emanates like a huge dunce cap from the aircraft's six o'clock. Most of the older heat-seeking missiles have to be launched into the cone of vulnerability. It is also the place where fighters going for gun attacks try to line up with their target's plane of motion.

Checking six is vital. Erich Hartmann, the Luftwaffe's top-scoring ace with 352 claimed victories, said that in 80 percent of his kills the victim was unaware he was under attack until it was too late. Although aircraft are now equipped with warning devices that indicate threats directed at them, there is still no substitute for having a wingman clear your six, or better yet, cranking your neck over your shoulder and checking it yourself. Seeing is believing. Eyesight cannot be electronically spoofed, nor can it malfunction at a critical moment. In the next war, all aces—in fact, all survivors—will have good eyes and sore necks.

In every contract there will be a separation of responsibilities, provisions for the change of tactical lead, target assignments, visual and radar search chores, duties for the engaged and free fighters, as well as a decision on when, where, and how to accept battle. There may be many versions of the same basic battle plan; the important thing is to *have* a plan and stick to it. Otherwise, mutual support is lost, wingmen are left hanging, and the effective fighting potential of the formation is cut to less than half. Improvisation has its place in air combat, but fighter pilots need a basic idea of what they want to accomplish and how they expect to do it *before* they enter a fight. The more thinking they can do on the ground, the better off they'll be in the air; in a dogfight there's barely enough time to react and almost no time to think.

Every contract carries with it a secret language, shorthand for commands and acknowledgments that the pilots use when flying and fighting. Most air combats follow roughly the same lines, at least in the initial stages, and two pilots who routinely fly together can say a lot in a few words.

They need to. In any future combat it is going to be hard to transmit more than two words at a time. There may be dozens of aircraft on the same frequency, all trying to communicate with *their* flight members. But the most important reason for using code words is the possibility—some would say the probability—of communications jamming.

The Soviets are very big on com-jam, probably because they realize how susceptible their own air operations are to such interference. Communications jamming can seriously degrade the effectiveness of an attacking force, but there are some things that can be done to counter it.

The first method is simply to ignore the jammer, who, in most cases, won't know he's effective unless someone says something about it over the radio. When the pilot gives a chattermark call—a command to change frequencies—the jammer knows he's on to something and starts "rolling," trying to find the new frequency, so it's best not to change unless it's absolutely necessary. Also, if the flight members keep transmissions short—code words—and transmit only when necessary,

the jammer has a hard time getting a radio fix long enough to be effective. Planning is also essential to combat com-jamming, knowing what information *cannot* be broadcast, and authenticating all new members of the net; the jammer's mission is confusion and delay, not espionage, but he'll take whatever pilots give him. The main thing for pilots to remember is not to lose their cool.

Ask any pilot what makes a good fighter jock and he'll say that besides having a good pair of eyes and hands and the ability to sustain a lot of Gs without losing situational awareness, the best pilots will always be the smartest pilots. They are students of the game, more artists than drivers. Every line pilot from Keflavík to Kadena knows the jargon, the attitudes, and the basic fighter jock skills, but the true air combat artist not only flies and fights, but thinks as well.

All the aces were not necessarily stick-and-rudder supermen; in fact there is evidence the great Red Baron himself had only slightly above average flying skills. But Rittmeister Manfred Freiherr von Richthofen, like Boelke, like Immelmann, like Galland and Bader, contributed something to the theory of air combat—a maneuver, a tactic, a *style.* They had a passion for flying and little else. They thought about it the way most men think of sex and money. They studied it as if more than just their lives depended on it. They were true students of the art of air combat and they never stopped learning.

A good pilot, a smart one, will have the ability to look at an opponent's plane and deduce what the bandit's energy state is, what he can and can't do with his aircraft. Similar to the way a veteran quarterback can "read" defenses, it comes from experience and study. By knowing what the enemy's aircraft is capable of at his current airspeed, altitude, and energy state, the smart fighter pilot can tell if the adversary is a threat or a target. The bandit may be in a dangerous spot, even behind and below him, but if he can't pull his nose up to get a shot off, he's not worth worrying about that particular microsecond.

Although good pilots have a knack for predicting what the other guy will do, they strive to keep their own actions unpredictable. They have a knack for coming up with things in the heat of battle, improvising solutions to problems that catch the enemy off guard and present him with a novel situation he can't handle. There are many stories from World War I in which outnumbered pilots turned to fight instead of flee, correctly assuming that separation would mean certain destruction but that accepting the attack would catch their adversaries off guard and give them just enough of an edge to survive and win.

Unpredictability is still important in air combat. The greatest North Vietnamese ace, Col. Nguyen Tomb, who shot down at least thirteen American planes (and who either "smoked Marlboros and drove a Citroën" or didn't exist, depending upon whom you want to believe), went hunting as number five man in a four-ship flight. Air Force pilots had been trained to see and keep track of even numbers of MiGs—they always travel in pairs, don't they? Well, usually. But most of Colonel Tomb's victims never saw him until it was too late because they weren't used to looking for the odd man.

Colonel Tomb was himself shot down by an unpredictable maneuver. A Navy F–4 pilot, Lt. Randy Cunningham, met up with Tomb on January 19, 1972. The two aircraft wound up in a series of vertical rolling scissors, with Tomb getting the best of it. Then Cunningham did the unpredictable—he cut his throttle and put out his speedbrakes, a tactic that would usually be a fatal mistake in combat with a more maneuverable aircraft such as Tomb's MiG–17. But because Tomb, low on fuel, was not expecting the unorthodox move, he overshot, giving Cunningham the separation he needed for a Sidewinder attack. His victory over Tomb was Cunningham's third that day, fifth in all, making him

and his radar intercept officer, Lt. (jg) Willie Driscoll, the Navy's only Vietnam aces.

Just as a fight between two skillful and evenly matched boxers will often end in a draw, a neutral nose-to-nose engagement between two pilots, equally skilled, flying equally capable airplanes, is usually inconclusive. If both pilots see each other, if all the systems are working correctly and neither pilot is low on fuel, if both pilots can sustain the same number of Gs, the victory will go to the pilot who can improvise a solution to the seemingly stagnant stalemate.

That's a lot of "ifs," and it usually never gets that far. Dogfights are lost, not won. Pilots are killed because they forgot to check their six and never saw what hit them. Pilots are killed because they were so intent on pressing an attack on one bandit that they didn't see the other one that shot them down. Pilots are killed because they neglected to check their fuel status until too late and either ran out of gas or were destroyed trying to separate. Pilots are killed because they misjudged either their own capabilities or the capabilities of their opponent's aircraft and pulled the wrong maneuver at the wrong time.

Aggressiveness *and* caution are the two most important qualities that must be instilled in young pilots. They are not mutually exclusive but rather two sides of the same coin; a pilot who is not a threat to the enemy *is* a threat to himself and his wingman, just as a pilot who is not cautious endangers everyone in his flight. This is a lesson that can be taught on the ground but learned only in the air. It is the basis of the Air Force's recent emphasis on realistic training.

In Vietnam, the USAF found itself with a rather disturbing kill-to-loss ratio; during some periods of the war it was less than one-to-one. Political restrictions had something to do with it. The lack of aerial targets and the overabundance of ground threats were also to blame. But training methods were also found lacking in preparing American aircrews to face the kind of air defenses encountered over North Vietnam. One of the surprising facts the Air Force learned in their "Red Baron" studies on air combat training was that experience seemed to have little to do with who was shot down in the air-to-air arena, but that the more experienced crews were likely to shoot someone else down. In the whole scheme of things, ground threats included, it was found that a pilot's chances for survival dramatically increased after his first ten combat missions. The USAF then went to work to try to find ways to simulate those missions in conditions as close as possible to the real thing.

The result was the Aggressor program. Following the Navy's Top Gun operation begun in 1969, the 64th Fighter Weapons Squadron was formed at Nellis Air Force Base in Nevada in 1972. The Aggressors did the Navy one better—instead of using F-4s (and occasionally A-4s) for adversaries as the Navy did, the Air Force practiced Dissimilar Air Combat Training (DACT), using T-38s and, later, F-5Es, which more closely approximated the small size and performance of Soviet MiGs. The Air Force also built the world's most extensive and sophisticated simulated ground threat environment for their Red Flag program at Nellis, once called "the closest thing to actual combat without getting shot at."

USAFE benefits from the new training program in two ways. In every fighter squadron there are graduates from the Fighter Weapons School at Nellis, who pass along what they've learned to the other pilots, keeping them up to date on the latest tactics and information. And USAFE has its own Aggressor squadron, the 527th Tactical Fighter Training Squadron at Alconbury. The USAFE Aggressors are constantly on the road, flying DACT missions against units throughout Europe, using F-5Es and Soviet-style tactics. Sometimes USAFE squadrons can't wait for the Aggressors to come to their base and go to Alconbury to hassle it out with the F-5s off the east coast of England. But the Aggressor's favorite hangout is Decimomannu, pronounced "dutchy-mo-MON-oh" and known throughout the command simply as Deci (pronounced "DUTCH-y").

Deci is an air base on the island of Sardinia, off the west coast of Italy. Fifty miles west of Deci is the Air Combat Maneuvering Range (ACMR), 700 square miles of the Mediterranean Sea studded with bright yellow and orange buoys almost fifty feet high. The buoys receive electronic impulses from pods carried on the aircraft, relaying them back to Deci where they are processed, and the fight is displayed on huge TV-like four-color screens. The exercise is recorded and can be played back to pilots from every angle with all the pertinent information—indicated airspeed, altitude, angle of attack, and so on—just as it was during the dogfight.

The Aggressors and the ACMR at Deci are invaluable training aids, but they are expensive and scarce. USAFE pilots can't get enough of them and usually wind up fighting each other for practice. This is certainly better than nothing, but leaves a lot to be desired.

For one thing, USAFE pilots are prohibited from flying at supersonic speeds below an altitude of 30,000 feet over land. This is a political necessity, but is a terribly constricting requirement and creates an unrealistic training environment for fighter pilots, who plan to go as fast as they can in any wartime situation. Pilots are also severely restricted in the limits of their temporary reserved airspaces (TRAs). The central European airspace is crowded enough; add to that the restrictions against overflying congested areas, bird sanctuaries, paratroop and helicopter exercise zones, balloon and glider space, and countless other "mink farms" (a nickname for restricted areas, coined in memory of an infamous lawsuit brought against the Air Force by an irate rancher who maintained the noisy jets were preventing his minks from making little minks). The TRAs are small horizontally, with altitude restrictions commonly from flight level 110 to 245 (11,000 to 24,500 feet). As one Bitburg fighter pilot complains, "It's like fighting in a closet."

But perhaps the biggest training restriction USAFE pilots face is their opponents, usually members of the same squadron because they're handy and a mission can be organized with a minimum of administrative hassles. It's not that the guys aren't good—in fact, they may be *too* good; it is unlikely F-15 pilots would ever run up against an aircraft as capable as their own, but being burned again and again by the Eagle's awesome performance could lead to some pilots being even more cautious than they need to be in a real dogfight against a much less capable airplane and pilot.

More realistically, there is a limit as to what can be learned from fighting the same pilots using the same airplanes and the same ideas day after day. USAFE pilots try whenever possible to fly against other NATO units. There is a mountain of paperwork to be moved for each such exercise, but both parties feel the experience is worth it.

Even with the restrictions imposed upon USAFE pilots, tactical air combat training is much more realistic now than it has been in the past. Slow-motion shadowboxing in a closet is better than not fighting at all. And if the rules cramp the fighter pilots' style, at least both sides are fighting under the same constraints. The rules of the game are not important as long as there *is* a game, because in any game there are winners and there are losers. Competition is the magic ingredient, the catalyst in the training alchemy. A steady diet of relentless competition is what separates the true fighter pilots, the real killers of the sky, from the rest of the air-to-air trout.

The USAF is not interested in filling its cockpits with a gang of steely-eyed government hit men weaned on hate and ideological fervor. Most pilots *are* politically conservative, but although that might have had something to do with why they joined the service in the first place, Air Force fighter squadrons have no dogma officers and no philosophic bed checks. It is more like a fraternity based upon the love of flying. What the USAF *does* demand of its pilots is aggression. This is the Air Force's word for it, but "aggression" in its most specific sense is not what they're looking for. The last thing any pilot needs in modern air combat is mindless belligerence; that will get him killed, along with his wingman and perhaps other members of his squadron as well. The kind of aggression the USAF wants is an attitude of invincibility, what football fans call a "winning tradition." They get winners through competition. Fighter pilots are drop-forged in the heat of competition—it starts on the very first day of training and it never stops.

"You see it a lot in ATC," says a USAFE fighter jock who was once an Air Training Command instructor pilot.

You'll take a guy up on his first formation ride. Supersonic, transonic, big jet, he's real excited, it's a T-38. He's scared to death because he's never flown so fast and so close to another airplane. He comes down, and he couldn't do it right but he really wants to do it. And the next day he's all excited and someday he becomes a fighter pilot.

Another guy comes down and his eyes are this big. He did poorly and he knows it—but they're expected to do poorly on their first ride—and the next time he goes up he's scared to death of it. He doesn't want to do it and he can't wait until the last day when he doesn't have to fly formation anymore. He'll never be a fighter pilot.

The competition never stops. Even in Bitburg the pilots are tested every time they fly. If anything, it gets harder and harder to win, because the higher up the ladder you go, the more winners you must beat to be number one.

"It's the ultimate goal, to go out and win," says a Bitburg F-15 pilot. "We're competitive animals. It's constant competition, and when you win you've got the champagne, you've got the laurels."

And if you lose?

"You get disgusted. You *try* to evaluate what you did wrong. It's a learning environment, everybody gets shot. We don't go off in a corner and sulk. Some people probably get very upset when they perform poorly, because they're very proud, vain people."

It is this part of the fighter pilot mystique that rankles other members of the Air Force community. To outsiders, fighter jocks are poor winners and even poorer losers. The constant competition convinces the pilots of their charmed status, that they will win the next contest just as they have won all the others so far, that bad things happen, but always to someone else, some *loser.*

"You have that superman feeling that you're sharp, you're good, you're going to cut it," says another USAFE fighter pilot.

They send ten aircraft out and only one's coming back, well, it's too bad those other guys aren't going to make it, because you're the one who's going to cut it.

It's kind of an arrogant, boastful attitude, so there's times you piss people off the way you act and stuff. But when it comes to the nitty-gritty, you *think you're going to survive. And I think if you* don't *feel, deep down, that you're going to survive, then chances are you won't go. You'll say, "It was fun in peacetime, but I'm a conscientious objector and I'm not going on this one."*

This artificially induced confidence sometimes manifests itself in braggadocio in younger or more insecure pilots. Although they would have you believe it is mere jealousy, nothing more, there is a reason other USAFE pilots have branded the F–15 jocks at Soesterburg and Bitburg "Ego Drivers."

"The ego is there," says a young F–15 pilot.

You could call it ego or confidence. You've never seen a quarterback go into a football game and say "I don't think I can win this game but I'm
going to give it my best shot." No, he says "I'll be damned, I'm just going to kick everybody's ass."

There's one philosophy that was explained to me by a guy that had a lot of experience. I was really concerned about something; we talked about this and we talked about that and finally he just looked at me and said, "You know, it's all just a damn attitude."

Exactly! A retreat into the inner world. How can you explain what it's like flying fighters to someone who has never done it? *Why bother to try?* Let them think what they will. The Air Force listens to fighter pilots, but the fighter pilots listen only to each other. The only opinion they acknowledge is the opinion of the other knights of the air, their true status jousted out almost daily on the cloudy quintains of the German skies.

Bitburg is not the end of the operational rainbow. The fighter ladder goes up, up into the heavens: the Aggressor squadrons, the Thunderbirds, the secret airfields out in the desert where Air Force pilots fly MiGs and stealth aircraft and God knows what else. But those positions take a lot of the right kind of flying experience, and to our young pilot there is no better place to pull down fighter hours than Bitburg.

He may get some static from the Navy Tomcat drivers out on Gonzo Station in the Persian Gulf, or the Israeli F–15 pilots of the Hyel Ha'Avir's No. 133 Squadron, or even—why not?—the flying officers of the MiG–23 *eskadril'ya* just across the border at Gross-Dolln. But our new tiger knows he has arrived. He is on his way to everything.

He stands motionless in the motion and noise. The squadron-issue Bitburger Pils in his trembling hand soon ceases its oscillation, the gyroscope of beer offering sure proof that *this place*—49°57'N, 6°33'E on your INS dial—is the center of his universe. Big Time! Bitburg! *Fighter Pilot Heaven!*

Right: F-15s of 525th TFS enter the break for landing; town of Bitburg is in the distance.

Fighter Pilot Slang

Fighter pilots everywhere have their own special language, and USAFE aircrew are no exception. Below is a short dictionary of air force slang that will help ordinary human beings decode these messages from the skies. Most of the expressions are not peculiar to USAFE but are used throughout the USAF (and the U.S. Navy and Marine aviation community as well). Remember, for better or worse, military aviation is a man's world, and fighter pilot lingo is pretty salty—but then, it was never meant to be written down and distributed to the public.

Ace-of-the-Base, Steve Canyon: A hot pilot, if only in his own estimation.

Airway Zombies: Eastern European airliners vectored through the air corridors to and from Berlin.

Bat Turn: A very tight, fast change of heading, used most often in F-16 squadrons. A reference to the rapid 180-degree Batmobile maneuver of the old Batman TV series.

The Big Surprise, The Big Contingency, Round Three, Day One/Wave One: World War III.

Blow his lips off, Shoot his shorts off, Hose him: The act of shooting down another aircraft.

Bogey Dope: Bearing, range, altitude, and number of unidentified aircraft.

Bravo Sierra: Bull Shit; the opposite of Sierra Hotel.

Brown Bar: Second lieutenant.

Check Six: Visually monitoring the aircraft's rear quadrant for enemy fighters.

Controller Mouth, Porky Pigging: Useless radio chatter.

Double-handed Polish Heart Attack: A last-chance evasive maneuver, sometimes referred to as the Violent Soviet Jink-Out or The Last Best Move.

Double Ugly: The F-4 (rarely used).

Ego Drivers: F-15 pilots.

The Electric Jet: The F-16.

Fangs Out: Going for an air-to-air victory to the exclusion of all other considerations, such as checking for other enemy aircraft.

Fighter Pilot Measles, High-G Hickeys: A rash caused by violent maneuvering, technically called petechiasis.

Fox One: A long-range missile attack.

Fox Two: A short-range missile attack.

Fox Three: A gun attack.

Fox Four: A mid-air collision (used only as a joke).

Furball, Squirrel Cage: A multi-plane, confused aerial engagement.

Gate: Afterburner.

The Golden BB: A relatively small caliber bullet that causes large problems in an aircraft; a lucky hit.

Gut Check, Belly Check: Rolling the aircraft to check for attacks from the aircraft's underside.

Hack: Capable of performing, e.g., "He can't hack the mission."

Hassling: Unauthorized, informal mock dogfight.

Hawking: Shadowing a three plane free-for-all at low altitude waiting for an opportunity for a quick, easy shot. Frowned upon by most pilots.

Head-mounted computer: The brain of a fighter pilot.

Hog, Warthog, Porker: The A-10.

Hummer: Any ingenious device whose proper name the fighter pilot can't recall.

Jock, Driver: Pilot.

Knife Fight: An aerial engagement where both aircraft are committed to a duel to the death.

Lethal Cone: The area immediately behind the aircraft's jetpipe into which most heat-seeking and gun attacks are launched.

Merged Plot: The point where the blips representing various aircraft are so close no further radar resolution is possible.

Mink Farm: An area that is a constant source of noise complaints.

Mud-Movers, Ground-Pounders: Air-to-surface attack specialists.

Mutual Support: The coordination of friendly aircraft in attack and defense.

Nines, Limas: AIM-9L Sidewinder missiles.

Nylon Letdown: An ejection.

Painfully Long Extension (PLE): Getting out of a fight at all costs, usually when Situational Awareness or Mutual Support is lost. Also expressed as, "Have no pride when it comes time to get the hell out of Dodge."

Pioneer Mode, Idiot Mode: Navigation system failure.

Pit: The back seat of a Tub.

Pitter, Prisoner of the Pit: The occupant of the back seat of a Tub.

Pucker Factor: The detrimental effect of having someone shoot at you while you're trying to deliver ordnance.

Punching Out: Ejecting.

Rippy: Rated Position Indicator Code; a high-ranking staff officer authorized to fly.

Sierra Hotel: Shit Hot; anything true, good, and useful. The fighter pilot's favorite expression.

Situational Awareness: A complete comprehension of the three-dimensional air battle. Very difficult, very necessary.

SLUF: Short Little Ugly Fella (actually, Short Little Ugly Fucker); the A-7.

Smash: Potential energy stored as a function of airspeed and/or altitude.

Spark 'Vark, Electronic Fox: The EF-111A.

Speed-o-heat: Very fast indeed.

Super, Outstanding: What fighter pilots say when they can't say "Sierra Hotel."

Switchology: Operating the various electronic navigational and weapons systems controls.

Tap, bounce: Unexpectedly attacking another aircraft.

Tiger Error: The detrimental effect of trying too hard to press an attack.

Tits Machine: A good airplane.

Tits-Up: Broken, not functioning.

Triple-A, Trip A: Antiaircraft artillery (AAA).

Tub: A two-seat aircraft, usually a trainer.

'Vark (Aardvark): The F-111.

Viper Driver: F-16 pilot.

Whiskey Delta: Weak Dick; a less-than-capable pilot, a wimp.

Whizzo, 'Gator, Fightergator, Backseater, Guy-In-Back (GIB), Ace of Gauges: Nicknames for Weapons System Operators.

Wild Weasel: The F-4G.

Wing Weenie: A member of the fighter wing's administrative staff.

Chapter 3
Interdiction: 'Vark Ridge

Kep. Phuc Yen. Thai Nguyen. Thanh Hoa.

They're on the map. Nobody remembers them. Nobody wants to remember them. To a nation trying to forget even the major North Vietnamese cities of Hanoi and Haiphong, the sacred airfields of Kep and Phuc Yen, the inextinguishable steel furnaces of Thai Nguyen and the unsinkable Dragon's Jaw Bridge of Thanh Hoa have already faded into oblivion.

But the U.S. Air Force remembers them. It remembers those places and a lot more you won't find on any map: The Hourglass Rivers. The Fish's Mouth. Death Valley.

And Thud Ridge.

In official USAF history, Thud Ridge is just a "nickname for a mountain range beginning about 20 nm. (nautical miles) north-northwest of Hanoi and extending about 25 nm. northwest, used for navigational and terrain masking, located in Route Package 6A."

But there's so much more to it than that. Thud Ridge isn't simply a geographic location. It's a state of mind, a place of honor and failure, a monument to bravery and unpreparedness. The world has forgotten Thud Ridge; the USAF cannot. The insignificant spit of rock and jungle still casts a

---

Lakenheath F-111F over the North Sea. The much-maligned Aardvark has performed superbly in the interdiction role for many years after a problem-plagued start.

---

shadow even on USAFE, fifteen years later and half a world away.

The USAF learned a lot in Vietnam, most of it the hard way. Current Air Force operational doctrine was forged in the heat of Rolling Thunder and Linebacker I and II. The modern strike package concept was hammered out in the skies above Route Pack 6. Almost every detail has changed since then, but the hard lessons learned over Thud Ridge have not been forgotten: Never go to war in the wrong aircraft. Never go to war with the wrong kind of training. Never go alone.

Many of the tactics vital to USAFE's mission were pioneered or perfected in Southeast Asia. The routine miracle of in-flight refueling was refined to an art. Techniques and equipment were developed for the new business of electronic warfare. The latest generation of precision guided munitions—"smart bombs"—were introduced in a wartime environment. Training programs were established to enhance pilots' abilities to survive and kill in a dogfight, a form of combat the USAF once thought obsolete and now considers routine.

And all the planes in USAFE's tactical inventory can also trace either their origin or development to the air war over Vietnam. The F-15 was born in the FX studies of the mid-sixties when the USAF recognized the need for a dedicated air-superiority fighter, a breed of bird that, if not extinct, was at least on the endangered species list with the F-4. The Phantom was itself changed by the war, going in as a Mach 2-plus, hard-winged all-missile inter-

ceptor and emerging as a somewhat slower—but quicker—dogfighter, with leading edge slats and a 20-mm Vulcan cannon in the nose.

Southeast Asia also painfully pointed out the need for a whole new type of aircraft, the electronic warfare and support platforms. The EC–121 College Eye airborne early warning aircraft and the EB–66C Brown Cradle ECM plane could barely handle the mission in Vietnam, but the lessons learned in their operational use were incorporated into the design of their successors, the E–3A AWACS and the new EF–111A, respectively.

The in-country support role was performed by a number of aircraft, none of which was particularly suited to the job. Armed transports, armed observation planes, armed trainers, World War II vintage medium bombers, and the most sophisticated supersonic aircraft in the world were all pressed into service for air strikes in South Vietnam. The results were poor to mixed, and the USAF soon realized that if it wanted an aircraft capable of performing the close air support mission effectively—and surviving, which was getting harder and harder to do in Vietnam, let alone the projected lethal environment of central Europe—it would have to build an airplane with the close air support role in mind from the ground up. The result was the Attack Experimental (AX) studies in the mid-sixties, culminating in the A–10, the USAF's first purpose-built close air support (CAS) jet and USAFE's dedicated tank killer.

Finding an aircraft to fill the interdiction slot was more difficult. Whereas just about any plane could have a go at the relatively safe "splinter missions" in-country with little risk to anything but trees, up north the communists were slowly building perhaps the most formidable antiaircraft defenses in the world. As the level of U.S. bombing increased, so did the numbers and sophistication of the North Vietnamese air defenses: Soviet radar-directed antiaircraft artillery, Soviet ground control intercept and early warning radars, Soviet MiGs and Soviet surface-to-air missiles were woven into an integrated system that was, according to American pilots who had flown in both wars, far more dangerous than anything encountered in "the barrel" over Germany during World War II.

When the Joint Chiefs of Staff ordered Rolling Thunder in 1965 and the air war over North Vietnam got under way in earnest, the USAF rummaged through its inventory to find an aircraft capable of surviving those deadly defenses and effectively performing the interdiction mission. As in the in-country war, the Air Force found just about every type of aircraft except the one that was needed. Like most superpowers, the United States had built for nuclear war. Conventional air warfare—dropping iron bombs, dodging flak, and dogfighting—was considered as obsolete as the Red Baron and the ring-and-bead sight. So when the USAF needed something to carry the big iron Downtown, it reached in its grab bag of nuclear bombers and supersonic fighters and came up with—The Thud.

The Republic F-105 Thunderchief is no beauty. With its area-ruled fuselage and stubby wings, the Thud looks, in planform, like a pterodactyl carrying a Coke bottle. Fully loaded, it took a takeoff roll so long it sometimes appeared as if the pilot meant to taxi the Thud all the way to North Vietnam. The hydraulic lines of the F-105's dual flight control system ran side by side, so a hit on one of them all too often meant a hit on both and the complete loss of control. Some planes glide in such a situation; the Thud dropped like a cement block, although a quick fix rigged up at their bases in Thailand gave the pilots a fighting chance to get the plane back over friendly territory before punching out. The F-105's maneuvering qualities also left a lot to be desired. "Even a Frisbee," it was said, "can out-turn a Thud."

It was a standard joke in Southeast Asia. Wherever F-4 pilots got juiced and loose, one stalwart Phantom flyer would always stand on the bar and yell, "What's the sound of an F-105 when it hits the ground?" The answer, delivered in a drunken, rousing chorus: "Thud!"

But the Thud had good qualities as well. It could carry more than twice the bomb load faster and farther than its Rolling Thunder stablemate, the F-100 Super Sabre. Hydraulics aside, the Thud could absorb a tremendous amount of damage and still make it home; it was not uncommon to see an F-105 return from a mission up north with gaping holes in its wings and a fuselage riddled with antiaircraft fire. But the best thing about the Thud was its speed, an inheritance from its birth as a supersonic nuclear bomber. The F-105 was, and still is, one of the fastest aircraft in the world where it counts—on the deck. Thud drivers soon learned there was no point in turning with the MiG-17 Frescoes, their low-level adversaries, when they could simply outrun them. Unless the MiGs could jump the F-105s before they had made their bomb runs, the North Vietnamese pilots usually gave up and went home. Unloaded and in capable hands, the Thuds were more than a match for the MiGs, or the Americans could simply refuse combat by lighting the afterburner and returning home at the speed of sound.

Eventually, the derisive nicknames—Hyper-hog, Ultra-hog, Iron Butterfly, Squash Bomber and, of course, the Thud—became terms of affection as the aircraft endeared itself to its pilots and gained the grudging respect of other fighter jocks. The

F-111F preparing to depart on training flight. Two-man crew sits side by side, pilot on left.

Thud flew over 75 percent of the missions in Rolling Thunder. The price was high. By the end of 1968 the USAF had lost over four hundred Thuds, more than half the F–105s in their inventory.

Thud Ridge was not the only ridge in North Vietnam. An outcropping of karst between the MiG base at Kep and Haiphong was sometimes referred to as "MiG Ridge," and there was even a half-hearted attempt to name something or other "Phantom Ridge." But Thud Ridge was the only name that stuck because it was the only one earned. The Thuds owned that real estate. The price was paid in aircraft destroyed, pilots cap-

tured or killed. The Thud was ready when called, performing a mission for which it was not built, with little or no support, in the most hostile environment ever encountered in the history of air warfare.

All this was not lost on the Air Force. When the air war began again over North Vietnam they were ready with new aircraft, tactics, and training. They went Downtown with a virtual armada of airplanes,

each with a specialized mission and all synchronized together in a strike package far more sophisticated than the rudimentary packages of the Rolling Thunder era. And even though the air defenses were even tougher, the USAF lost proportionately fewer aircraft and crews.

But the moral of Thud Ridge is not how to fight the Vietnam air war over again. On the contrary, the lesson the USAF has learned is not to expect any particular kind of war and to be ready for all kinds, from counterinsurgency all the way to the Big Contingency itself. The Air Force has acquired, at great effort and expense, an inventory of specialized aircraft, building blocks from which it can

F-111F viewed from KC-135 tanker, with its variable-geometry wings in forward position.

construct a strike package to execute virtually any type of mission.

There was a time when multirole fighter bombers like the F-4 were thought to be the answer, but the increasing sophistication of enemy air defenses, both in the air and on the ground, has led to increasing specialization. That the FX and the AX programs were conceived almost simultaneously was no accident; the F-15 and A-10 are

complementary aircraft, each optimized to perform its specific role to a degree of effectiveness that could never be achieved by any multimission fighter bomber.

Even the Thud's successor, the General Dynamics F-111, has been rescued from the multimission miasma. The USAF, who knew better, started the whole mess themselves back in 1960 with the Tactical Fighter Experimental (TFX) studies, when they sketched out plans for the most advanced strike aircraft in the world and called it a fighter. Since the Navy was looking for a new fighter, Secretary of Defense Robert McNamara dragged the Navy and the Air Force together and lectured them on how much money could be saved if they both adopted the TFX.

All of this brings to mind President Coolidge's sole surviving witticism: When badgered about new airplanes for the fledgling Army Air Corps, an exasperated Silent Cal replied that perhaps they should just buy one plane and take turns flying it. The problem was that the fighter the Navy wanted and the fighter the USAF wanted were two completely different airplanes. The fighter the Navy wanted was a fleet defense aircraft, a real dogfighter with the added capability of firing very long-range missiles to protect their task forces from cruise missiles. The fighter the Air Force wanted was, quite simply, a bomber, and no amount of program management, no matter how brilliant, was ever going to pull the two together.

But they tried. McNamara was very serious about the TFX commonality concept, and the Navy went through three programs—the Weight Improvement Program, the Super Weight Improvement Program and, in a fit of military sarcasm, three separate Colossal Weight Improvement Programs—before it became clear, even to Secretary McNamara, that the F-111B, as the Navy version of the TFX was called, just couldn't handle the mission.

The Navy eventually got its fleet defense aircraft, the Grumman F-14 Tomcat. That the F-14 has a great deal more in common with the F-15 than with the F-111 shows, in retrospect, how misguided the idea of TFX commonality was in the first place.

The USAF got what it wanted, too: the F-111. But its problems had just begun.

Ostensibly to test and evaluate their new aircraft under operational conditions, but really to silence political sniping at the F-111 project, the Air Force rushed six F-111s to Southeast Asia in a program called Combat Lancer. The program was a disaster; three of the six aircraft were lost almost immediately. The cause, discovered much later, was not enemy fire, but a problem in the tailplane that caused the plane to go out of control. (A similar problem, with an entirely different cause, resulted in a ten-day grounding of General Dynamics F-16s in 1981.) The loss of half of the first operational deployment of the F-111s, followed by their grounding for another, unrelated problem—fatigue cracks in the wing carry-through box, the massive hinge the wings swing upon—only convinced the

F-111's many critics in the press and in Washington that the aircraft was a lemon.

But the F-111 was, and is, a sound aircraft. F-111 aircrews eventually overcame bad luck and bad press by returning to Southeast Asia and tackling missions no other aircraft could consider performing. The F-111s went Downtown, back to Hanoi and Haiphong, again and again, alone, at night, and in the weather. Slowly, the awkward looking airplane with the swinging wings and the long snout began to win friends.

Like the F-105, the F-111 had picked up a lot of nicknames in its misunderstood adolescence. General Dynamics had wanted to call it the Lancer, after a series of nicknames begun with their Delta Dart and Dagger series, but the name never caught on. Australia, the only other nation to operate the F-111, calls their C model the A-8 Kangaroo. The North Vietnamese, one of the few groups who realized the plane's potential, called it "Whispering Death." The F-111 has also been called the Swinger, Snoopy, and the Switchblade, but the name that stuck is the one coined by F-111 pilots in Southeast Asia: the Aardvark. Like the Thud before it, the Aardvark's most vocal supporters, even in the darkest days of its development, were the pilots and weapons systems operators who risked their lives flying the F-111 in combat.

"The airplane does it," says an F-111 driver at Lakenheath.

It did it in Vietnam with the old A model. That's what scares the bad guys, because in the worst kind of weather we can go hit them and they can't hit us. They know from ten years ago when the F-111s were flying over Hanoi and they weren't able to touch them.

Aardvark whizzos share their pilots' confidence in the airplane. The F-111 has perhaps the most sophisticated avionics package of any aircraft in the USAFE tactical inventory and depends upon its electronics to survive: The terrain-following radar guides it automatically at altitudes, speeds, and in weather conditions that would be suicidal in any other airplane, and the F-111's complex navigation and threat-warning systems allow it to deliver ordnance in the most hostile environments. With the new Pave Tack laser bombing system being introduced in some USAFE F-111s, the WSO's already heavy work load has been increased to the point that it's probably the most demanding job in the USAF navigator field. It's also one of the most sought-after positions in the Air Force. An F-111 whizzo is not just along for the ride, and there's a long list of navigators who would love to get in the right seat of an F-111.

"The F-111 is the plane to be in—definitely," crows an Aardvark whizzo. "There's a lot of difference for the navigator career field, getting in an F-111, strapping one on at 250 feet and 600 knots, as opposed to a C-5 navigator hauling Dixie Cups to La Paz."

So the story has a happy ending. The F-111, which started life as a fighter that was meant to be all things to all people, has emerged as a dedicated strike aircraft, the most capable tactical bomber ever built. The later versions—the F-111Es at Upper Heyford and the F-111Fs at Lakenheath, the most powerful Aardvarks ever— are probably what the Air Force had in mind all along. But the F-111 still lugs around three hundred pounds of angle iron in its tail to accommodate carrier landings, a legacy from its days as a Navy orphan. If the Aardvark is still occasionally misunderstood in the United States, its usefulness is all too clear to the Soviet Union; it was the only aircraft specifically mentioned by the Russians in the first round of the Strategic Arms Limitation Talks, in which it was considered a "strategic" weapon.

F-111 drivers still call themselves fighter pilots, but as the 20-mm Vulcan cannon is systematically replaced by the Pave Tack laser guidance pod in the F models, the last vestige of air-to-air romance is slowly being stripped from the F-111.

"I like to believe I'm a fighter pilot, but I'd probably be one of the first to admit it's a bomber airplane," confesses the vice commander of an F-111 squadron at Lakenheath. "It was built to do all missions, and it soon became apparent that it could not do all missions well, although it could do a couple of missions extremely well."

The mission the F-111 does extremely well is interdiction, penetrating behind enemy lines to bomb ground installations, supply dumps, and communications. For NATO, the two most important interdiction targets are the second echelon of troops marshalling behind the front, and airfields, a type of interdiction mission sometimes called counterair.

Executing an interdiction mission in the dense and deadly air defenses of central Europe will take a strike package far more complex and specialized than even the most baroque strike packages of the later Linebacker operations. Vicious as were the SAMs, MiGs, and flak over Hanoi, Route Pack 6 would be considered almost a low-threat environment compared to some parts of contemporary eastern Europe. In Vietnam, the USAF fought the students. In Europe they would have to fight the teachers. The Soviets are the world's most zealous practitioners of the art of antiaircraft defense, and they've had a good ten years to dream up more black trash to throw at American pilots.

"A package is really something to put together and a lot of people don't realize the scope," says an F-4 backseater. "They're one little cog in the wheel."

In any USAFE strike package, the first planes in and the last planes out will be the recce birds, the reconnaissance aircraft, taking before and after pictures of the target to assess the defenses and the damage. Reconnaissance is a dangerous mission, flying alone and unarmed over hostile territory with speed the only defense. The USAF pioneered the use of remotely piloted vehicles (RPVs) in Southeast Asia, and RPVs will probably

see action in the recon mission in any future war in Europe.

RPVs are hard to pick up on radar, hard to hit with antiaircraft fire and are, according to Soviet sources, "absolutely fearless." The Israeli Air Force used RPVs to help take out hostile SAM batteries in the summer 1982 air war over Lebanon. But in some cases there will always be a need for a "head-mounted computer" in the cockpit, to make judgments no computer can handle, and USAFE RF-4Cs from Alconbury and Zweibrücken could well be the first American aircraft to cross the line in any future European war.

The main body of the package, the strike flight, could consist of any aircraft capable of dropping a bomb: USAFE F-4s, and F-111s, NATO Buccaneers, Jaguars, Mirage Vs, F-104s, and, soon,

Left: F-111F tanks from Mildenhall KC-135 over the North Sea. Aardvark can take on 10,000 pounds of fuel in under five minutes.

Above: Two-ship of 'Varks over Scotland, prior to descent for low-level mission.

Tornados. The F-16s at Hahn would be outstanding in this role. The F-16's dogfighting ability has been widely publicized, but in Europe—and Israel—Fighting Falcons are considered even more valuable in the ground attack mission. Although it lacks the range and payload of the F-111, USAFE's premier interdictor, the F-16's formidable self-defense capability and state-of-the-art avionics have led to some amazing accomplish-

63

ments; in a recent RAF-sponsored bombing competition, a team of F-16s finished first, with 98 percent of the maximum points possible, a perfect bombing score on all four days of the exercise, fewer valid SAM (surface-to-air missile) launches than any other team, and—this is the part that has old F-4 hands spooked—the F-16s "shot down" eighty-eight of the fighters that were sent to intercept them, without jettisoning their bomb loads and without ever resorting to fuel-guzzling afterburner power. The F-16s suffered only one kill during the entire competition. The other teams averaged almost three losses per mission.

To support the strike flight, the USAF has built a number of dedicated electronic warfare aircraft. Wild Weasel F-4Gs from Spangdahlem will suppress enemy radar-directed missile defenses while, farther back behind the lines, the new EF-111A Electronic Fox (already dubbed the "Spark 'Vark") jams enemy GCI and early warning radar and the EC-130H Compass Call jams communications between enemy aircraft and their controllers.

The E-3A AWACS will provide the strike package with early warning of enemy air defenses, while an orbiting EC-130 airborne command post will copy in-flight reports from the recce forces and help direct the air battle. Farther back, the tanker cells will be ready to stuff the returning strike flight with much-needed fuel, while a RESCAP force of planes and helicopters will stand by to rescue crews of downed aircraft. Most of the auxiliary elements and parts of the strike flight will be protected by fighter escorts, still called MIGCAP, in spite of its unambiguous derivation.

The USAF has invested a huge amount of money, time, and effort in its new generation of EW—electronic warfare—support aircraft. They are preparing for a war of electrons, a war they think this time they will win. That was another hard lesson learned at Thud Ridge. (The Israelis learned their lesson over the Suez in 1973, and taught a postgraduate course to the Syrians in 1982.) In order to survive, let alone triumph, in a modern hostile environment, effective electronic warfare doctrine and hardware are absolutely vital.

The Soviets have long been interested in electronic warfare and are considered to be more advanced than the West in some EW aspects—jamming battlefield communications, for example. They call it "radio-electronic war" and fight the battle across the entire electromagnetic spectrum, from radio frequency (RF) and infrared to sound and sonar.

Critical as it is in the modern air combat arena, electronic warfare is often misunderstood and dismissed as tangential by the press and public. It's hard to grasp why control of the electromagnetic spectrum is so important.

Let's start with radar, the most contested battlefield in electronic warfare. Air forces depend on radar to locate enemy planes (and friendlies), to direct missiles, to deliver ordnance, and for navigation. They are, quite simply, blind without it. Never mind for now how you keep your eyes open. How do you poke the other guy's eyes out?

Here's what a pilot and an electronic warfare officer of an F-4G Wild Weasel at Spangdahlem have to say about electronic warfare. Like their namesakes, Wild Weasels hunt their prey by using themselves as bait. Specifically, their wartime mission is to suppress enough of the estimated 4,300 radar-controlled SAMs in the Warsaw Pact to allow the strike flight to get in and out safely. The F-4G is the long-awaited successor to the F-105F and F-105G Wild Weasels pressed into service in Southeast Asia.

Here's an electronic warfare briefing from two guys who should know:

"It's not very hard to trick a radar, because it's electronic and very sensitive," the pilot explains.

It's like your transistor radio; it's electronic, too, and all you do is rub your hair and put your hand on your radio, and it'll screw up. You can throw

toilet paper out there and it will jam the radar just as good as chaff—especially if it's Danish toilet paper.

His electronic warfare officer picks up the narrative:

The problem with radar is you transmit X amount of power over X amount of miles and the dissipation is incredible. They're putting out a million watts, and what hits your airplane might be a hundred-thousandth of a watt. Now it's got to bounce back into the radar set. So the power loss between bouncing off a surface and getting back to the system is just tremendous, it's one times ten-to-numbers.

When you're jamming something you don't have that problem. It's a one-way thing, so it doesn't take nearly as much power. That's something

Mark 20 cluster bombs await loading onto Lakenheath F-111Fs.

people don't realize; they say, "Now how are you going to trick this thing that's on the ground and it's big as a house and it's got all this power?" Well, you don't have to trick it. You can out-power the thing. The Radar Reflectivity Formula is a real player in a game like that.

There are inherent limitations of radar that cannot be overcome. Radar is not the be-all and end-all, but so far nobody's come up with anything better than radar to direct a missile. They'll keep improving, but the line of sight restriction will always be there. So will the size restriction—the

smaller you make a missile, the shorter its range gets. This isn't to say these things aren't any good. If you don't watch what you're doing, any one of them is going to hose you. We're going to lose a lot of airplanes.

If the Wild Weasels go to war, they will carry out their suppression mission in one of three ways: They will blow a hole in the missile belt to allow the strike flight to get through the line, they will escort the strike flight all the way to the target and back out again, or they will go out autonomously and search for mobile SAM sites to knock out on a hunter-killer mission.

The Wild Weasels describe an average mission:

We would decide what our area of interest is at an altitude and a range where we can't be intercepted. We need line of sight on the radar, so we'll pop up to an altitude where we can work signals, but we won't stay at that altitude. We'll get the electronic order of battle; see what's there and

Aardvark, a solid but less-than-beautiful bird, here strikes an elegant profile pose high over the North Sea.

where it is, what we're going to work and what we're going to suppress, and let them see us. We have the advantage of knowing exactly where the enemy defenses are with our equipment, we know when they're shooting at us, and as soon as they see us, we see them.

As we get closer to where we're going to work we drop down and maybe go off in a different direction or go hide for a few minutes. Then we come back and, basically, the EWO puts the pilot in a position to shoot the missiles at the target. Based upon our priorities—what poses the greatest danger, who is the most worthy of getting destroyed today—they pop up on our scope and we say, "There's a likely candidate."

But how do the Weasels keep from popping up on the bad guys' scopes? How do they avoid getting shot down by the very missile batteries they're assigned to suppress? Nothing is guaranteed, but here's a Weasel scouting report on Soviet battlefield missiles and the Weasel's game plan to elude them:

The (SA-) 2, 3, and the 4, their big problem is their size. Anything that's big, like a big airplane, it's not very maneuverable. And the 2 and the 3, they're old—anything old can't fight, just like old people.

With the 4, no doubt, they envisioned a high-altitude threat from our intercontinental bombers. Well, we fooled them; we're going low, and that is reflected in their later systems, which all have an improved low-altitude capability.

The SA-6 was a very successful missile in the 1973 Mideast conflict (although the Israelis clearly had its number by 1982). *It's the closest thing to our Hawk, but then again it's Russian technology. That's the biggest weakness of all these missiles, they're Russian technology. To defeat it—I guess I can say that—anybody who knows anything about radar knows that the radar looks for motion, primarily going away or coming at you, so you weave in side to side.*

The SA-7, that's an IR (Infrared) missile. You have to see that one because you're not going to hear it, there'll be no electronic indications. The 7 and 9 have the shortest range, you can outrun them.

The 8 will probably be the big killer because it's small, it's state of the art—not much smoke. The way you avoid it is the way you avoid somebody's punch; you just wait till the last second, till you can't stand any more, then you move. The best defense is to see the missile.

If you can put something between you and the missile, it ain't going to hit you. They do have some memory, but not much. Some missiles have a guidance radar that has you illuminated, so the missile doesn't necessarily have to see you. Putting something between you and the guidance radar will cause the missile to go ballistic. You can hide behind a hill. You can hide behind trees. All you have to do is break the radar's line of sight.

To be successful, the Wild Weasels don't necessarily have to kill anybody. If the missile batteries shut off their radars to avoid emitting signals for the F-4Gs AGM-45 Shrike and AGM-78 Standard ARM (antiradiation missiles) to home in on, or if the batteries can be kept so busy shooting at the F-4G that they leave the strike flight alone, then the Wild Weasels consider their mission a successful one.

Unlike the Weasels, the strike flight won't stick around to joust with the air defenses. They'll come screaming in as fast and as low as they can get. USAFE strike pilots sometimes fly at close to Mach 1 and 250 feet—the peacetime limit—and all say they'd go even faster and lower in wartime: "We're going to be down there with the tanks and trucks," says an F-4 pilot, "especially crossing the FEBA" (Forward Edge of the Battle Area).

F-105 pilots in Vietnam used Thud Ridge to break the radar line of sight, but later in the war the USAF developed electronic countermeasures (ECMs) against the old SA-2s and flew in discrete ECM formations—"resolution cells"—at medium altitudes to stay out of reach of the ferocious ground fire.

That won't do in Europe: "At medium altitudes," says one Phantom jock, "you're going to get killed." So the Americans have reluctantly joined their NATO allies groveling down in the weeds, at "fifty feet and the speed o' heat."

There are a lot of reasons for going in low. One of them is the use of terrain masking, hiding behind hills and houses to break the radar's line of sight. Another is the difficulty enemy fighters would have spotting the strike flight skulking along near the ground. (This is why ground attack planes are camouflaged and aircraft that work at high altitudes, the F-15 and the AWACS, for example, are not. There was once a move afoot to paint the F-16 in "European One" camouflage, the "Lizard" finish used on the A-10. It would certainly have been more effective in the interdiction role than the "Ghost Gray" air-superiority scheme now used on the aircraft. But the Fighting Falcon flyers, who would much rather think of themselves as "fangs out, stick aft, hair on fire, and press on with a bat turn" fighter jocks than mere air-to-mud ground-pounders, revolted en masse and the idea was quickly shelved. F-15 pilots have a similar revulsion to the new F-15E Strike Eagle, the dedicated interdictor version of the F-15, also painted in Lizard colors. They like the plane okay, but they hate the *idea.*)

But even if the enemy fighters picked up the low flying strike flight, there's not a lot they could do to stop them. Flying low deprives the attacker of the use of the vertical plane for energy. Conversely, the thicker air at low altitude is more conducive to evasive maneuvers in the lateral plane—a slatted F-4E is at its best in this situation.

More importantly, most air-to-air missiles have a much smaller envelope, or no capability at all at ultralow altitudes due to the difficulty the infrared or radar seeker head has in picking up the target aircraft against the false returns from the ground, called "clutter." This is why developing fighters and missiles with "look-down, shoot-down" capability is so difficult and so vital. The F-15 has some look-down, shoot-down capability. So does the new version of the MiG-25, the "Foxhound," according to some sources. But until the considerable problems are worked out, SAMs and AAA, not fighters, will continue to be the strike flight's biggest worries.

Even if a pilot hears the dreaded call of "Vampire!" meaning a SAM has been launched at his aircraft, he still has a good chance of breaking the lock and avoiding a "nylon letdown"—or worse. Strike fighters go through the Weasel's bag of tricks: jinking, hiding, out-turning some missiles and outrunning others.

Most USAFE planes also use ECM—electronic countermeasures—to frustrate the guidance systems of infrared and radar-directed threats. Some aircraft, like the F-15 and most Navy planes, carry their ECM gear internally, but on the majority of USAFE strike aircraft it's hung outside on the bomb and missile racks in ECM pods. Although this creates drag, especially on the return trip when the plane would be zooming home otherwise unloaded, the USAF feels this is more than compensated for by ease of maintenance and the ability to swap pods from one aircraft to another.

Aircraft also carry chaff, either stored internally or externally in pods or packed into speed-brakes, used as a last resort to break enemy radar locks. They use infrared countermeasures as well—flares, hot gas, or flashbulblike blinkers—to spoof enemy IR missiles designed to home in on the heat put out by the aircraft's engines.

But ECM can itself be thwarted by electronic countercountermeasures.

An aircraft can jam a threat radar by radiating excessive electromagnetic power back to the radar receiver. When the enemy radar operator looks down at his CRT expecting to find an aircraft neatly "painted" on his screen, he sees instead an asterisk-shaped burst of RF activity. He knows the blip is there somewhere in that starshell pattern, but it doesn't do him much good—he needs to know exactly where the target is to aim his missiles or vector his fighters against it.

Or does he? Many modern missiles have a home-on-jamming feature and will automatically seek out and destroy the source of radar noise. And many modern radar sets are "agile"—at the first sign of jamming they will automatically begin transmitting on a different frequency.

One counter to agile radars is barrage jamming, transmitting jamming power across several frequencies, but this takes an enormous amount of power and is usually reserved for larger, more specialized planes, like the AWACS. A more elegant solution is deception jamming, making the radar believe the aircraft is somewhere where it isn't. This is done through a highly complicated process called range gate stealing—"capturing" the radar return signal from the aircraft's skin (actually masking it in a higher powered signal generated from the ECM equipment) and beaming it back at progressively slower speeds. At 600 knots, a delay of a fraction of a second will cause the missile to miss its target or deny the radar-directed AAA a valid tracking solution.

There are countermeasures to deceptive jamming, too, just as there are ECCCM to ECCM, all the way to infinity. It's a giant chess game out there, moves to countermoves, and it never stops. Although any one threat can usually be countered if the pilot is aware of it, it's the combination of threats, the saturation, that has USAFE pilots worried.

The Soviets have thousands of SAMs and AAA batteries deployed throughout central Europe and they rarely replace an old system with the new one. This doesn't mean they aren't making new SAMs—they are up to the SA-teens now, as a matter of fact—but they keep the two systems out in the field side by side. Even the old SA-2 Guideline, scourge of Vietnam and the Mideast, is lurking just across the line.

And even if they never shoot anybody down, just the sheer numbers of antiaircraft defenses will make USAFE aircrews nervous. It has been estimated that the effect of being fired on by AAA, no matter how inaccurate, will reduce the accuracy of the attacking aircraft by as much as 50 percent, especially in older aircraft with predominately manual bombing systems. This is known as the "Pucker Factor" and is the real reason behind antiaircraft defenses—not to shoot down aircraft, although that's a good way to do it, but to degrade the effectiveness of the air attack.

Keeping tabs on the various threats—guns, missiles, and fighters—each with its peculiar envelope, guidance system, and nasty habits, coming at different altitudes and airspeeds from mobile sites, fixed sites, and foxholes, is getting to be too much for a human mind to handle. The pilot has enough on his mind flying at supersonic speeds, dodging telephone poles, and dropping bombs. Even if he sees this one and that one, he'll probably never see the other one, the one that gets him.

For this reason, the latest generation of ECM suites and pods is completely automatic. All the pilot has to do is turn it on, and the system will analyze and counter any threat directed at the aircraft. Since the system uses a computer for power management, it can be "taught" new threats simply by changing the software.

Computer-assisted power management is the latest word in electronic warfare, but it is far from the last. There will be counters to it, and counters to the counters. Electronic warfare is the hottest battle of the cold war; the struggle goes on every day between Silicon Valley and the Zhukovskiy Academy, with skirmishes in West Germany, Japan, and the United Kingdom. The Soviet Union tries hard, spends lavishly, but lacks the technological base—especially in microprocessors—to make any real advances and is forced to spend much of its effort countering the latest American breakthroughs in electronic warfare. The United States, on the other hand, is working on the leading edge in most airborne electronic warfare research, but sells, gives away, or is robbed of most of it.

If, as someone said, World War I was a war of brawn and World War II was a war of logistics, then World War III, should it occur, will be a war of electrons. The USAF has learned the lessons of Thud Ridge; it stands prepared in Europe and hopes, by being prepared, to never have to learn the new and terrible lessons of the Harz Mountains, the Hindu Kush, or whatever they will call "Vark Ridge" in the next war.

Chapter 4
Close Air Support: The Golden BB

The Soviet commander-in-chief is relaxing in Brussels after his troops have taken Belgium. He turns to the Soviet Air Defense Minister and asks, with a cat's smile, "Tell me, Comrade Marshal—who did win the air war?"

Like most World War III jokes, this story told by a British general is not particularly funny, but it proves a point—air power alone will never win a war.

"To win a war you've got to occupy ground, and that's the Army's job," says an F–4G Wild Weasel electronic warfare officer.

Our mission is support. The F–15s can shoot down thirty MiGs and we can suppress a hundred sites, but if the strike flight doesn't drop their bombs on the airfield it's an unsuccessful mission. If some F–15 goes chasing some guy and allows ten other guys to go in and dick the strike flight, then he hasn't done what he's there for. It's the A–10, F–4, F–16, and F–111 that drop the bombs that are going to be the winners as far as the Air Force is concerned.

The Army and the Air Force both agree the main uses of air power are to neutralize the opposing air forces and to support the ground troops in the land battle. But they have disagreed, sometimes violently, on the order and relative importance the two missions—counterair and ground support—should have.

There have been interservice rivalries since there have been separate branches of the services, but nothing like those that have existed in the U.S. military. The Air Force entered World War II as the Army's stepchild, but emerged as king among the services, so favored and powerful it could dictate peace terms to its mean Army stepfather, which is just what it did in the postwar conferences that realigned the American military. The new USAF got everything—sexy fighters, mighty bombers, and ominous nuclear missiles. The Army was allowed only light prop planes, and almost as an afterthought, those curious new noisemakers called helicopters.

Maybe because they didn't trust the Air Force to take care of them, and maybe because they wanted to grab a little of the glory that goes with the wild blue, the Army almost immediately set about arming their helicopters. The first use of helicopters on the battlefield was in the Korean War. The fragile choppers did surprisingly good work as flying ambulances, but even then there emerged the now-familiar sight of some grunt sitting by the door with his machine gun ready to go.

At first, the Air Force reacted with smug amusement. After all, they had the fighters, and there's something about a fighter that makes otherwise responsible governments want to buy them in-

---

Left: Fairchild A-10 Thunderbolt II at RAF Bentwaters. Note off-center mounting of GAU-8A Avenger 30mm cannon.

71

Portable gun loader, powered by A-10's internal hydraulics, can upload a full complement of 1,100 30mm rounds in minutes.

stead of buying tanks, or spare parts, or even hospitals. But the Army kept developing helicopters, and in the Vietnam War the choppers really came into their own. The price was high. The Army lost at least four thousand helicopters, perhaps more—like most Vietnam terms, "loss" meant anything the Army wanted it to mean, and some sources say that if even so much as the tail fin could be salvaged a new machine would be built around it, the loss converted to mere "damage."

When the Department of Defense squashed, once and for all, the Army's attempt to defend itself with fixed-wing aircraft (the sneaky grunts were hanging ordnance on their OV-1 Mohawk observation planes), they started to develop purpose-built helicopter gunships.

The Air Force wasn't too worried about the Army's first attempts, regular UH-1 Hueys with door guns and grenade launchers. But when they got a look at the AH-56 Cheyenne they got downright apoplectic. Here was a machine that looked like a *fighter!* It looped and rolled and went faster than any helicopter ever went before. Underneath its huge bubble canopy were "electronics more complex than those of the B-52." It had a curious upside-down tail, retractable landing gear, and more firepower than many Latin American armies. The Cheyenne looked like a fighter and fought like a tank.

The Air Force saw the writing on the wall. The Cheyenne project was abandoned in 1969—after the Army had signed for 375 AH-56s the year before—ostensibly because the Cheyenne was just *too* complex. If this was the real reason for ditching the program it would be rare for any American service, and it is interesting to note that when the Air Force's Attack Experimental (AX) program was begun back in 1967 the AH-56 was very much alive.

Perhaps this is a bit cynical. As we have seen in the previous chapter, the USAF fought the in-country war with every kind of aircraft but the kind that was needed—a purpose-built close air support plane capable of carrying huge amounts of ordnance low and slow enough to deliver it effectively and tough enough to take hits and still get home. And since the USAF's pride and joy, the FX air-superiority fighter was, for the first time in a long while, not designed for dropping bombs, they needed a companion aircraft that could be built relatively cheaply and in large numbers to complement it.

The Air Force had been taking a lot of flak in the press over alleged mismanagement of their aircraft development programs (they saw it∙as a popular misconception of the inherent dangers of working out on the leading edge) and hoped to get a breather with a comparatively "low-risk" plane like the AX. But they took great care to see the AX program was well run.

The USAF started at the bottom, examining the close air support role in great detail and taking nothing for granted. They seriously considered biplanes and for a while it looked as if the AX would have propellers. In fact, the Mohawk was very close to the way the Air Force first envisioned the AX, sort of a cross between the OV-1 and the Skyraider.

As the Air Force saw it, the prime mission of any close air support aircraft is to kill tanks and other enemy vehicles—although the AX was designed in the Vietnam era, even the Air Force knew *that* couldn't go on forever and that central Europe was where the aircraft was most likely to be deployed.

They decided to build the AX around a gun for several reasons: The ranges at which most American PGM (precision guided munitions) and air-to-surface missiles work best are also the optimum ranges of most enemy SAMs and AAA. But new technology made it possible to design a gun that could penetrate a tank's armor, especially the less-thick side and rear armor that only an aircraft can get at. Besides, cannon shells are much cheaper than bombs and missiles, and the aircraft can carry more of them.

So the AX was built around the GAU-8A Avenger cannon, a huge 30-mm seven-barrel Gatling gun that fires shells the size of milk bottles, made of spent uranium—they are not radioactive, but they *are* very, very heavy, giving them high kinetic energy and contributing to their penetration power. The linkless feed system allows the gun to spew out up to 4,200 rounds per minute.

Once they had the gun technology down, the AX designers went about building an airplane around it. They closely examined the reasons for losses of close air support aircraft from ground fire in the Vietnam and Mideast wars. They found most of the losses—62 percent—were caused by fuel fires and explosions. Accordingly, the four fuel tanks in the A-10 are widely separated, filled and surrounded by fire suppressant foam. The wings are almost dry, with only two small tanks nestled up against the fuselage, their contents drained by taxi, takeoff, and flight to station. The two main fuel cells are also filled with reticulated foam and are protected by the airframe armor. The fuel pipes are self-sealing and check valves prevent fuel from flowing into a ruptured tank, while firewalls prevent engine fires from spreading to the fuselage.

The second largest cause of losses was damage to the aircraft's engines, flight controls, and airframe structure. Accordingly, the engines, which look as though they're stuck on the A-10 as an afterthought, are actually well placed. Not only does their high position minimize the danger of foreign object ingestion when taking off from rough strips, but their separation keeps a hit on one engine from being a hit on both.

The flight controls are triple redundant; that is, there are two sets of primary hydraulic controls and a manual backup. Cables were used for the control runs because research showed they are less easily jammed in battle than are rigid rods. The two systems are spaced widely apart, meeting only in the cockpit to avoid both systems being knocked out by the same hit.

The whole construction is rugged (Britain's premier aviation writer, Bill Gunston, writes, "Americans always use the word 'rugged' here, though this word actually means 'rough, hairy and uneven' "). The wings, tailplane, and fins are all built around triple spars, and coupled with other protection, it is said by A-10 pilots that the aircraft could lose one engine, half a tail, two-thirds of a wing, and parts of the fuselage and still fly.

But no plane can fly if the pilot is dead, and 18 percent of the losses the designers examined were chalked up to pilot incapacitation. So one of every ten pounds of the aircraft's weight was given to armor plating, most of it devoted to protection of the pilot, who sits in a titanium "bathtub" that surrounds the cockpit. Developers fired 23-mm high explosive and armor piercing rounds straight at the "armored bathtub." The armor was "discolored," nothing more. Higher caliber 37-mm HEI (high-explosive incendiary) rounds were also shot at the armor; it was slightly dented, but again there was no penetration. The ammunition drum is similarly protected with armor and placed as far as possible from the skin of the aircraft.

The aircraft's camouflage scheme is another example of the effort the AX designers devoted to making everything exactly right. They started from scratch—after all, the USAF had no experience in painting battlefield jets. Their first efforts were shades of gray, dozens of them. They tried light grays, including ADC Gray, Gull Gray, and Airframe Gray (very light shades close to those found on old Navy and Air Defense Command aircraft). Then they went to darker shades—Gunship Gray and Dark Ghost Gray, like the darker gray of the F-15.

These worked well in theory, but in practice the pale A-10 "sausage" stood out prominently against the thick green forests of central Europe. The designers went back to the drawing boards and came up with the mottled green and gray European One, the "Lizard" camouflage now on the aircraft.

One of the early test schemes (along with polka dots and see-through black paint) was "40% Reflecting Mask 10A," a special paint that reflects 40 percent of the light that shines on it. The paint was designed to reduce the A-10's infrared visibility, and the color changed with the light. The European One A-10s seem to change color from shade to sunlight, suggesting that perhaps some of the reflecting qualities of the experimental paint job have found their way into the current camouflage scheme. The way the "Lizard" appears to shimmer at times, perhaps it should more appropriately be called "Chameleon."

The A-10 was also one of the first aircraft to have its red, white, and blue national insignia replaced with the new low-visibility black outline, the current standard. Gray fighters like the F-14 and the F-16 have gray insignia outlines, and even the F-111s at Lakenheath are beginning to go to the black star-and-bar. Curiously, USAFE's first-line air-superiority aircraft, the F-15, still retains its full-color national insignia.

The result of all the research was the A-10 Thunderbolt II. The slow, awkward-looking aircraft resembled anything *but* a thunderbolt, and was quickly dubbed "Warthog" by its pilots. It may look thrown together, but it's a carefully designed airplane.

But will the Warthog work?

"There's no doubt in my mind that the A-10 is a survivable airplane," says a USAFE A-10 pilot.

You talk to A-1 drivers after one tour in Vietnam; I'm sure they got shot up numerous times and brought that hog back without any sweat.

It makes us feel real nice that the A-10 is so survivable. But then again, if you think real hard about it, if they made it this survivable, maybe this sucker's going to take a lot of hits.

The A-10's natural enemies at low level are much different from those that threaten regular fighter pilots. Hog drivers don't have to worry much about MiGs and telephone pole-sized SAMs arching at them through the blue.

The SAMs they worry about are little suckers, short-ranged but very lethal. The SA-7 Grail started it all. When the small, shoulder-launched infrared SAM was introduced, it changed the face of low-level air combat. Popularly called the Strella, or "arrow," the SA-7 chased away many aircraft that had no business being on the battlefield.

But it's getting old now—the SA-7 can be outrun or spoofed and its small warhead doesn't pack much punch. A larger missile, the SA-9 Gaskin, is now carried on a BRDM amphibious wheeled vehicle. Even the SA-9 is being replaced by the SA-13, which has already been reported operational in East Germany. The SA-13 has an infrared seeker that operates in two colors—really two frequencies—to frustrate target countermeasures.

But the most vicious low-level SAM is the SA-8 Gecko, once called "the closest Soviet equivalent to the European Roland," high praise indeed. Two radar-directed SA-8s are usually fired simultaneously on different frequencies to make spoofing more difficult.

A-10 drivers are also worried about guns, specifically, the many and terrible ZSU-23-4 radar-directed antiaircraft guns. With its rapid-fire four-barrel cannon and Gun Dish radar, the tracked, armored Shilka, as the ZSU is sometimes called, wreaked havoc among low-flying Israeli planes in the Mideast wars. Although it runs through ammunition at a prodigious rate, and although American ECM is said to have the Gun Dish's number, the "Zip-Gun" is the Warthog's mortal enemy.

But like all low-altitude pilots, the A-10 drivers worry most about the "Golden BB."

"Trip-A (antiaircraft artillery) accounted for 95 percent of all the kills in Vietnam," says an F-4 backseater.

Only 5 percent were MiGs and SAMs. And that was at medium altitude.

When you think of AAA, you normally think of something you see on the runway, but when I think of AAA, I think of you getting drafted and they give you a gun because the war just started and you go out there and say "Look, there's an airplane!" and you point your gun up and you shoot. You take a couple million soldiers coming in one direction, all sticking their guns up in the air and shooting at once and you've got a real threat, because you're going to find those folks anywhere.

That's the "Golden BB," the unlucky strike that incapacitates aircraft and pilots. A-10 jocks try not to dwell on it too much because there's not a lot they can do about it. They're too busy dealing with the antiaircraft professional to spend precious time worrying about some free-lancer in a foxhole taking potshots at them with an AKM assault rifle.

Most USAFE strike pilots can find some consolation in speed, decreasing their exposure to enemy fire. But the A-10's lack of speed is legend. ("The A-10 is the only aircraft that suffers bird strikes from its six o'clock," chuckle fighter pilots.) Warthog drivers take solace instead in the fact that the AX designers tried to make the plane "Golden BB-proof."

"The F-4 drivers—or fast movers, we call 'em —their motto is 'speed is life,' which is true in their business and their realm and their aircraft," says a Hog driver at Sembach.

So a lot of people coming out of Phantoms don't think the A-10 will survive. I personally have been used to flying low and slow when I was a FAC (Forward Air Controller), and a lot of former FACs —OV-10, A-1, T-28 drivers—are flying the airplane and enjoy flying the airplane and believe that it will be a survivable airplane.

So the fast movers believe that we're just going to get hosed, big time. And our thought is, yeah, we're probably going to get hosed, but so will they, and at least I will be closer to friendly troops than them. When they get hosed they'll be seventy miles back.

For any aircraft to survive in the dense, low-level antiaircraft environment of the modern battlefield, it will take coordination and teamwork. And for all the Bravo Sierra talk about helicopters versus the

OV-10 forward air control and observation aircraft lands at Sembach, Germany. Green camouflage is replacing grey paint jobs. USAFE operates OV-10s without back-seaters in most missions.

A-10, they work best together. At the Joint Attack Weapons System exercises (JAWS I at Fort Benning, GA, JAWS II at Fort Ord, CA), it was discovered the loss rate went down and the probability of kill went up dramatically when USAF A-10s and Army helicopters worked in concert.

The helicopters and the A-10 complement each other very well. Helicopters can do things airplanes can't—they can hover out of sight, popping up just long enough to take a quick look around or get off a shot. And they are very stable weapons platforms, especially for antiarmor weapons like the wire-guided TOW missiles that have to be steered by their operator to the target. But choppers are fragile and are limited in what they can carry—no helicopter gunship, for example, can carry the two-ton Avenger cannon and the six Maverick missiles the A-10 carries.

The A-10 and Army helicopters work together in a Joint Air Attack Team. This JAAT is controlled by an Army "battle captain" in a scout helicopter and an Air Force forward air controller, either airborne in his own helicopter or an OV-10, but more than likely on the ground.

The Air Force learned a lot about forward air control in Vietnam and have taken it to heart. Most of the Sembach personnel are trained FACs. Some of them fly OV-10 Bronco aircraft, but most of them are posted with Army units all over Germany, calling in air strikes from jeeps and armored personnel carriers crammed with sophisticated communications gear. The USAF would probably like to have all its FACs airborne, but the unarmed Broncos would be easy targets for modern battlefield defenses. They are instead designed to orbit behind the lines and relay messages from ground FACs to strike aircraft and mission headquarters. This is why most of the two-seat "Lizard" OV-10s are usually flown solo in Europe.

"I guess during the war the way they plan it is the guy in the backseat's going to be plotting the data for you, and the guy in the front will be flying the airplane, avoiding the threat," says an OV-10 pilot. "That's the plan, but I think it's going to end up you're going to be the only guy in the airplane going out there. They're not going to have the spare bodies just to throw in there."

The first thing the Joint Air Attack Team leaders will do is call in artillery fire to spread confusion among the enemy and keep them "buttoned up," unable to use the heavy machine guns mounted on their turrets. Artillery may also fire illumination rounds to confuse IR missiles.

The helicopters use "nap of the earth" tactics, almost scraping the ground, and exposing themselves to fire only when attacking. Staying at maximum range, they concentrate on the dreaded Shilkas and SAM units. They never pop up in the same place twice, and often scout helicopters draw the fire of the defenses while attack helicopters sneak in a quick shot.

Meanwhile the A-10s, in loose two-ship "double diamond" formations, come in low, masked by the terrain. They also keep their exposure at a minimum, but they'll be coming in too fast to pick and choose specific targets.

If I pop up over a ridge line and there's four things out there—an APC, a ZSU, a tank, and a truck—50 percent of the time I can't tell you which is which because in the heat of battle I'm not going to sit there and say, "Okay, which one is the tank?" To hell with that—if I see something, I'm going to put the cross on it, squeeze the trigger, and then break off. If it's a tank, great. If it's not a tank, great. The longer time you spend on final, straight and level, the greater the chance of you getting shot down.

A-10 pilots open fire at a range of about 2,500 feet and cease fire at about 1,500 feet. Firing at a greater range reduces the chance of hitting or penetrating the target, wastes ammunition, and churns up smoke and dust that make it more difficult to aim correctly. Firing at shorter ranges is particularly unpleasant because of the "pyrophoric" effect of hits from the Avenger cannon, seen as a jagged, white explosion of melting armor caused by 30-mm shells that have the angles necessary to penetrate.

The A-10 can also carry the full range of Air Force air-to-ground ordnance but the pilots would rather not. To deliver iron bombs and cluster munitions they would have to fly over the target, and their survivability, according to one A-10 pilot, depends upon stand-off weapons—the gun and the AGM-65 Maverick missile. The Maverick is

77

DANGER
EJECTION SEAT

electro-optically guided; the pilot selects the target on his TV cockpit display and the missile homes in on the picture he's selected. (Actually, the missile doesn't "see" a tank, it only sees the contrast in a selected scene, so it's effectiveness can be degraded by poor visibility, darkness, and smoke. An imaging infrared Maverick now under development will relieve some of these problems.)

The gun is *loud.* The standard USAF air-to-air Vulcan 20-mm cannon sounds like a foghorn, but the A–10's Avenger gun goes off with a deafening double burp, the "echo" caused by the rounds breaking the sound barrier.

Above: A-10s are fully instrumented and now carry inertial navigation gear, but most Hog drivers prefer heavy doses of map reading.
Right: A-10 front office. Yellow handle fires ejection seat. Note multiple weapons release buttons on stick.

It works, too. There's a piece of thick steel plating on a desk at DET 1 headquarters at Sembach. It used to protect an acoustic scoring device at a French gunnery range—used to, that is, until an A–10 blew it apart on a training mission. At practice ranges in England, A–10s routinely uproot logs supporting the targets.

Above: A-10 was literally designed and built around the two-ton GAU-8A Avenger cannon.

Even though they pound the ground, even though their helmets are covered with camouflage tape and they would rarely fly above the treetops on a real mission, the A-10 pilots still call themselves fighter jocks. They have a right.

"Most of the guys when they go through DM (the A-10 training program at Davis Monthan Air Force Base) do air combat tactics," says an A-10 "fighter pilot."

I did them against F-15s, other guys do them against F-5s or A-7s or A-4s or stuff. Up at high altitude they hosed our butts, but down at low altitude we had a lot of fun.

Everybody likes to jump A-10s because they go very slow. They think, "Here's a piece of meat on a platter." But after they've tried it a couple of times and realized we could turn on them faster than they could turn on us, they re-evaluate their thinking.

There's two kinds of airplanes—they're either turners or accelerating-type aircraft. So when an accelerating-type airplane attacks an A-10, what he needs to do is use one type of tactic, and if it's a turning airplane you use another type of tactic. They were trying to slow down and turn with us, which of course gave us a tremendous advantage on them.

Very rarely do I ever come close to the aircraft's (G) limitations; don't need to. All fat-wing aircraft

have a better turn capability than thin-wings. Fast movers with their wings swept back have got to pull higher Gs to maintain the turn radius, or turn rate, than I have to do at a lower G. So, with most of the aircraft that we're dealing with, 5 Gs will be sufficient to put him in a position where we can defend ourselves.

Does this mean A–10 pilots have to worry about MiGs, too?

"If they're there and they see us, if they've got the gas and nothing else to do, sure they'll come after us."

But what about enemy helicopters?

If they're at my twelve o'clock, we're firing. If they're in the target area and we're working, say with Army helicopters, and the enemy helicopters come in there and are putting a threat to us and

Above: Spent-uranium rounds are loaded at high speed into A-10's ammo drum. Extreme heaviness of bullets generates tremendous kinetic energy upon contact with armor.

---

the other helicopters, no doubt about it. I come up over the ridgeline and they're there—BRRUUFFF! —they're taking the big schnitzel.

The Marines have developed antihelicopter tactics for their cannon-armed version of the Bronco, the OV–10D. And the Luftwaffe Alpha-Jet, which can carry Sidewinder air-to-air missiles, was at first thought to be valuable in this role, although the idea has since been scrapped. But the A-10 jocks have enough on their hands without trying to be antihelicopter heroes. Ultra-low-level flying and fighting, dodging hills and houses, and navigating

by map and the seat of the pants is fatiguing. The work load on an A–10 pilot in combat approaches the saturation point.

"We do have a very heavy work load, but what you have to do is space it out," says an A–10 pilot who's been in Europe for a while.

We'll go in there and beat up the target for a few minutes, get out of the target area, take kind of a breather, sneak in from another direction, come in and hammer them again.

I think if you don't *take a breather you'll have one mission—actually half a mission. You'll take off, beat them up for a while, and get shot down. You just can't stay at a high level of concentration over an extended period of time, especially if you're yanking and banking your airplane around and have the airspeed and G available and the*

Above: A-10 maintenance at RAF Bentwaters. Note off-set nose gear to clear enormous gun. Main wheels retract only partially into wing pods, facilitating emergency wheels-up landings.

total concept of what's happening and where you need to be.

A-10 pilots got some relief from their heavy work load when an Inertial Navigation System (INS) was introduced into the newer models of the aircraft, but some old Warthog hands don't like it:

I think, personally, that it will make the pilots a little worse at visual navigation, because you can, if you're not aware of it, slip into the mode where you're just following the needle like all the other fast movers. They get down low, and they're not

Above: The Warthog, although graceless, is a potent and unparalleled performer.

used to map reading—and they've probably got a one-to-a-million map, anyway—and they just follow the needle. You punch in the INS and it's really neat—except when those electrons go squirrelly and then you find yourself in some place that, one, you don't know where you are, or two, you shouldn't be there.

It will be extremely helpful, especially in bad weather situations, but you always have to be aware that it can go tits-up, just like anything else, and when it comes between trusting myself and the map and this thing, well, I'm going by the map.

Even with the inertial navigation system, the A-10 is still a clear-weather aircraft. It seems odd that the AX designers, who were so careful about designing the aircraft, overlooked the environment in which it was designed to fight. Is the lack of an all-weather capability really important to the A-10? Listen to a Central European weather report by an F-111 driver at Lakenheath:

If you look at any kind of graph about the European theater, it's darkness or in the weather 80-plus percent of the time. In wintertime around here, what time does the sun come up and go down? It comes up about eight and goes down about three or three-thirty. So two-thirds of the day is night, and when the sun is up, it's pissing rain.

Because of this, and because the A-10 accident rate is somewhat higher than projected, possibly because of a lack of Warthog trainers, there is talk of building two-seat A-10s. A special Night/Adverse Weather Warthog is under development with forward-looking infrared sensors, multimode radar, radar altimeter, laser ranger, and the new INS. Like the F-15, the A-10 was designed to accommodate a second cockpit with little structural modification. Some critics say the Night/Adverse Weather A-10 is the plane the Warthog should have been all along, but Congress wanted the A-10 to be a cheap program, so the extras were built in later to make the aircraft more capable—and more expensive—bit by bit.

Since the A-10 pilots are used to driving by road map, the low-level landscape that is just a blur to regular Mach 2 fighter jocks is Hog Heaven to them:

Since we're lower than most of the other fast-movers, we get into it. If I say "Meet me at the Twin Towers" they know what I'm talking about. Or I'll say, "Meet you at Donnenburg (mountain)." Or "Meet you down at Low-Fly Seven."

Left: A-10 can be gassed for rapid turn-around from a single fueling point.
Above: A-10's turbofan engines are set high and far apart to increase survivability.

Right now, I could throw my maps away and I could get my airplane anywhere from Nürnberg to north of Frankfurt without getting violated in peacetime or without getting shot down in wartime.

Much has been made of the A-10's ugliness. And compared to sleek, swoopy fighters, the Warthog *is* outclassed. But handsome is as handsome does, and to a bunch of hardpressed grunts trying to fend off an enemy armor attack, the graceless planform of an A-10 would be a welcome sight indeed.

"I think it's probably the ugliest airplane we've built," says an A-10 detachment commander. "It's also the meanest-looking. It's a very business-looking airplane, especially when you're looking down the barrel."

Chapter 5
Air Defense: Merging Plots

Our job is deterrence, to be a contender to the point that they look across the fence and say "Nope, not today."

We call it a gorilla when we get a bunch of airplanes together, and they are going to come over in a whole zoo, I think.

Our job is to turn them around—shoot them down before they get here.

They are the Threat, the Aggressors, the Bad Guys, the Bandits, the Big Red Machine, the Crimson Tide, or—to call *them* by their right names—the air forces of the Soviet Union and the Warsaw Pact. These USAFE pilots are careful to use the universal menacing pronoun, but even official directives about "nonspecific nationalities" cannot mask the fact that the greatest potential threat to their security is just a quick MiG ride across the border.

We have seen in the previous chapters how USAFE will cross the line on interdiction missions and how they will operate on the battlefield in the close air support role. Now we'll examine USAFE's role in air defense, clearing the central European airspace of hostile aircraft in any future war.

Air defense is a part of a larger mission, counter-air, which includes attacking enemy airfields and flying air-superiority missions across the line. Air defense shoots down intruders with SAMs, AAA, or fighters, or it may take a passive form, like dispersing the aircraft and hardening their shelters, while camouflaging the bases from the air.

Left: Aggressor F-5E at RAF Alconbury; note Soviet-style nose numbers. The small F-5 approximates the look and performance of the MiG-21.

Above: Aggressor pilots rehash tactics. Patch of the 527th Aggressors at Alconbury.

The other NATO allies contribute to the air defense effort, of course. But the United States and the European nations differ in air defense philosophies: While the rest of NATO rely heavily on SAMs and AAA, USAFE depends more on fighters. The different philosophies have their good and bad points: SAMs, and especially AAA, are cheaper and can be operated by less-experienced personnel. But they are relatively immobile, especially when compared with fighters.

The United States and the other NATO nations also differ in the way they employ their SAMs. Almost every central European NATO nation contributes to the Hawk Belt, a line of SAMs that runs north to south through West Germany, about thirty miles west of the East German border. But the United States is the only nation that deploys its Hawks in depth, making it more difficult for attackers to blow a hole in the belt or to saturate the system.

The sites are interdependent, controlled as a NATO asset even in peacetime. They are also constantly on the move, with one site's movement always covered by another. But the destruction of a few key sites could negate the whole system. This is especially true in northern Germany, where the thin Hawk Belt is stretched tightest. There is a similar missile belt, comprised of high-altitude Nike-Hercules sites, paralleling the Hawk Belt about fifty miles back. But the Hawk is NATO's first line of defense.

Some defense critics say NATO lags behind the Soviets in surface-to-air technology, pointing to the sheer numbers and types of SAMs in the Warsaw Pact inventory. But the fact is, the West doesn't need that many SAMs—the Hawk is that good.

The HAWK (or Homing-All-the-Way Killer) was born in 1954 as a U.S. Army requirement for a surface-to-air missile system capable of traveling with the Army in the field and engaging targets at low level. It was a very far-sighted concept for the times, and almost every allied nation soon signed up for the system. An improved version of the MIM-23 missile was developed in the late sixties with a larger warhead, improved guidance, and more efficient propellant. This I-HAWK (Improved HAWK) forms the backbone of the NATO missile belt.

The Hawk has its problems. It is hardly mobile in the modern sense of the word—a Hawk battery on the move looks more like a modern rock band on tour than a SAM battery on deployment. And it is expensive. (The newest American SAM, the Patriot, does with one phased-array radar what it takes Nike-Herc and Hawk batteries nine radars to do. However, like most modern systems, the Patriot is *ungodly* expensive.)

But the Hawk works—it had a probability of kill greater than 90 percent in Vietnam and the Mideast Wars. Just how good is the Hawk? Here's what a Wild Weasel electronic warfare officer, USAFE's resident expert on SAMs, has to say about it:

I think it's the best missile system in the world. I'm glad it's on our side. It's a very automated system, it doesn't leave a lot to chance. With the Soviet systems, there's a whole lot of operator technique, and those folks don't shoot a whole lot of missiles at a whole lot of airplanes.

But what about the Hawk's lack of mobility?

It's a defensive system—we don't plan on attacking them, we plan on them attacking us. And when you're on the defensive it gives you a lot of advantages when you're building things. You can't go one to one when you're attacking somebody, you've got to go four or five to one. It allows you to put things into a system like the Hawk that you couldn't put in a system that you wanted to take out to the field.

The first thing you can anticipate they're going to do is send every plane they can get to bomb our airfields, so you want a system that is ready to shoot missiles at those hundreds of airplanes. If they do their job and the airfields are protected, then they've done just about the best job they can do. *We don't want them out there with the Fifth Corps when we go attack Poland—they're there to knock down that zoo on Day One of the Big Surprise. The way I think that zoo's going to come over the line, they're going to lose a lot of airplanes. I honest-to-God think we're going to run out of missiles on those sites, and they've got a lot of missiles out there.*

The American SAM sites are run by the U.S. Army, but like the rest of the missile sites in the NATO Hawk Belt they are controlled by NATO, along with the Quick Reaction Alert aircraft and various radar sites, under the NATO Air Defense Ground Environment (NADGE). This is NATO's most effective cooperative achievement to date, a network of missiles, AAA gun sites, fighter interceptors and radar installations from the Mediterranean to Iceland.

Operational control for NATO offensive missions is invested in the Allied Tactical Operations Center (ATOC). There are two centers in 4 ATAF, one at Sembach and another at Messtetten. There are two ATOCs in 2 ATAF as well, one at Kalkar and the other at Maastricht, at 2 ATAF's wartime headquarters in the Netherlands. The defensive missions, including the Zulu flights, are controlled by NATO Allied Sector Operations Centers (ASOC). A typical ASOC operates out of a "Rubber Duck," a huge, inflatable dome that shelters fourteen control scopes for radar operators and seven vertical plotting boards.

The GCI—Ground Control Intercept—officers are called controllers and specialize in either offensive or defensive missions. They are also known by other names. One full colonel once reportedly called them "dregs of the Air Force."

This is typical. Fighter pilots have no use for anyone but fighter pilots. And although even *they* agree GCI can literally mean life or death, they don't like to admit it. In Vietnam, fighter pilots sometimes accused the directors of "Porky Pigging," or having a bad case of "Controller Mouth" —talking too much, cluttering up the radio nets with useless chatter, blasting pilots off the air with their huge ground-based transmitters. And this sometimes happened, especially when the overworked controllers suffered from fatigue. But for each of those cases, there was another one in which a controller saved a pilot's life, getting him to a tanker when he was low on fuel or vectoring rescue forces to a downed fighter.

There may be a darker side of this. Many of the controllers are women. It is the closest they come to combat in the USAF, the nearest they get to the fighter pilot's world, and they are beginning to feel the heat. Women are now allowed on the AWACS, although they were excluded for a while. In fact, there was talk that the entire weapons controller field would be closed to women.

The USAF regards women the same way fighter pilots feel about their backseaters: They are fiercely loyal to the female controllers they know personally but ambivalent about them as a breed.

"We've got quite a few women in the ATOCs, and we're reaching a point now where it's starting to give us some problems, simply because of the numbers and the physical work involved," says a high-ranking officer at Sembach.

Technically they're very qualified, some of our best people as weapons controllers and maintenance people, but they just can't hack the physical labor. And when they get pregnant they're out for thirteen, fourteen months.

The commander of a radar installation, who says he "couldn't do it without my gals," tends to be a little more philosophical about women in combat.

We are, as a nation, having trouble defining what the role of women is. I think rather than being an individual decision, it's more of a cultural decision, and until that decision is made, every single time something like this comes up someone's going to have to sit down and make a decision: "Is this combat or is this not combat?"

Until the armed forces come up with some valid criteria of what combat is, there will continue to be a case-by-case evaluation that threatens to keep

experienced female weapons controllers off the AWACS and allows Army secretaries to work on the East German border. If any inference can be drawn from the U.S. military's past definitions of the role of women in combat positions, it is this: They will continue to be allowed to serve in positions where they can be killed, but never in any position where they might defend themselves.

Pilots have more substantial reservations about ground control than just sexism. They say it is pointless to train under such rigid GCI control when it is not likely to be available in wartime. They are wary of becoming too dependent on ground control, especially when the GCI sites will prob-

Ground Control Intercept scopes and boards in portable "Rubber Duck" shelter. Radar transmitters are remotely located and linked by microwave.

ably be jammed or destroyed at the first outbreak of hostilities.

But a good controller, if he—or she—has the time and skill, can be an invaluable aid to the pilot. At Nellis AFB, under admittedly unrealistic optimum conditions, controllers are more "Nonflying Wingmen" than "Scope Dopes." A good controller can give "Bogey Dope"—bearing, range, altitude, and number of bogeys—as well as vector the fighter to an advantageous position. At "merged plot"—when the fighter blip and the bogey blip meet on the radar screen and no further resolution is possible—the fighter will call a "Judy," meaning the fighter pilot has the bogey on his own radar and wants control of the intercept.

Whether or not the ground-based radars can be jammed or destroyed is problematic. But Allied ground-based radars would certainly be prime targets in any central European war. The radar sites do what they can; they intend to move at the first sign of hostilities and keep on moving (except for the fixed German site at Wasserkuppe, almost within mortar range of the East German border—"How long you'd have that hummer in a wartime situation is anybody's guess," says a Master of Understatement at Sembach). The radar antennae are widely separated from the installation and connected only by a microwave beam, so if enemy antiradiation missiles take out the radar dish, the equipment and crew will be spared, and when a new antenna is erected, the unit will be back on line.

But there's one limitation that ground installations cannot overcome. They are limited in range to a specific formula (the square root of the radar aerial height multiplied by 1.22 plus the square root of the altitude of the aircraft being detected multiplied by 1.22). No operational air defense radar can see over the horizon (although high frequency surface-wave radar under development can) and the lower the targets fly, the more the range is reduced, allowing low-flying planes to pass undetected or reducing the reaction time to dangerously low levels.

In 1963, the USAF began to investigate the feasibility of using look-down radar to detect low-flying targets. The result was the E–3A Sentry Airborne Warning And Control System (the term AWACS is really a generic term like fighter and applicable not only to the E–3A, but the Navy's Hawkeye and the RAF's Nimrod as well. But the words E–3A and AWACS have become synonymous in the public's mind and are virtually interchangeable except in specialized publications).

The first E–3A became operational with the 552nd AWACS Wing at Tinker Air Force Base in 1978. The wing's three squadrons—the 963rd, 964th, and 965th (there is a fourth, training squadron, the 966th)—are still the only units flying the E–3A. But while it is based in Oklahoma, detachments from the 552nd operate on TDY (Temporary Duty) all over the globe and are frequent visitors to USAFE bases.

The E–3A is the most advanced collection of technology flying; it is also the most expensive. As we have mentioned before, the range of a radar is a function of the height of its aerial. But at a normal operating height of 40,000 feet, the E–3A has an effective target detection range of over 250 miles, a range so great that in wartime the E–3A would take off from bases in Germany and fly west to take up station.

The AWACS's trademark, the thirty-foot skunk-striped rotodome, rotates six times every minute on station, but spins at only ½ rpm during takeoff and landing to prevent low temperatures from congealing the lubrication. Its AN/APY-1 radar is so powerful the crew must shut it off two miles before tanker rendezvous or risk igniting the tanker's fuel load with microwave emissions. The radar and associated 4 Pi Model CC-1 computer can track and plot hundreds of civil and military aircraft; the E–3A has often surprised crews of civilian airliners operating far from land with its awesome tracking capability. It is said the radar can instantly pick up enemy aircraft taking off behind the line, as opposed to forty or fifty minutes for ground-based radars.

NATO is now receiving its own AWACS. The first of a planned eighteen NATO AWACS has been delivered from the final assembly plant at the Dornier Reparaturwerft at Oberpfaffenhofen. Many of the components are made in Europe under coproduction deals, but the program is still frightfully expensive, a fact that has led to much discussion and delay.

The NATO AWACS will be registered in Luxembourg for political reasons but will carry predominately German crews and will be based at Geilenkirchen, near Mönchengladbach and the "Clutch" Royal Air Force, Germany bases. Some NATO AWACS will be based on the flanks. The NATO AWACS were to be the first aircraft to have NATO markings—the compass star insignia and "NATO" and "OTAN" on its wings and fuselage. But, due to legal considerations (NATO is an organization, not a country), the NATO AWACS are now scheduled to sport the brand-new insignia of the Luxembourg Air Force, a red lion on a blue and white roundel.

The NATO AWACS will also have the improvements being incorporated into the latest USAF Sentrys coming off the line, including a new computer that operates three times faster and has five times the memory of its predecessor. The improved AWACS also has an enhanced maritime surveillance capability and new communications equipment, including the latest secure radioteletype system.

The AWACS carries four flight crew members and thirteen AWACS mission specialists. It is relatively plush inside (especially when compared with other USAF 707 variants) with carpeted floors, a galley, a rest room, finished bulkheads, six bunks, and sixteen airline-type seats in the rear. The latest AWACS has completely replaced the old cathode-ray-tube consoles diplaying raw radar returns with new alphanumeric displays on nine consoles. There are three more consoles planned for the E–3A, and when they are installed the crew will lose its "Picnic Area," a large carpeted space in the rear where the "crew dogs" now sprawl out on the carpet for a rest.

The USAF makes it a point to have a general aboard the E–3A in times of crisis to make the potentially far-reaching decisions a system like the E–3A sometimes forces upon its commanders.

The AWACS has revolutionized modern air combat, but its true capabilities are often not understood by the public. A single Sentry on a north-south racetrack orbit along the western border of West Germany can vector friendly fighters against low-flying intruders, steer friendly strike flights around hostile fighters, transmit tracking data to SAM sites, delineate divisional boundaries and status from transponder-equipped jeeps, and send and receive vital information to other NADGE (NATO Air Defense Ground Environment) members.

And the AWACS is mobile, invaluable in filling gaps in coverage left by the destruction of a radar site or in trouble spots where there are no ground-based radars. The AWACS can also enhance the coverage of the ground-based radar systems by expanding and updating their picture (the AWACS speaks a data-link language, called TADIL and pronounced "Tattle"). Fighters can maintain radar and radio silence while the AWACS vectors them against bandits through a data-link. The E–3A's look-down capability, coupled with the F–15's awesome climb rate, can actually vector the Eagles *up* from low-level hiding places to intercept intruders, an amazing new wrinkle in the air-to-air arena.

The AWACS' importance in modern air combat is hard to overemphasize. Even the smaller, comparatively less sophisticated E–2C Hawkeye changed the balance of power in the Mideast, chasing Syrian Floggers out of Lebanese airspace by steering Israeli Air Force F–15s and Kfirs to advantageous interception positions. Nobody knows more about the importance of AWACS than the Israelis, and it's no wonder they objected so strongly to the proposed sale of AWACS to Saudi Arabia. Although the AWACS carries no weapons, it is far from a purely defensive system, no more than generals like Rommel and Patton could be considered "defensive" generals just because they never personally shot anyone on the battlefield.

But the AWACS has its drawbacks. It is, as we have mentioned, budget-bustingly expensive, and a loss of just one AWACS would be a major defeat. They are more like capital ships than aircraft—in fact, that's one of the problems. The Navy has been accused of spending too much of its resources protecting its carriers from attack with too little left over for other missions, and this could also apply to the USAF and AWACS. One of the Germans' initial arguments against the AWACS was the reported belief that it would take as many as 120 fighters to protect a single E–3A. The aircraft carries no weapons, but like all 707 derivatives, the E–3A has a hard-point under its port wing, usually used for carrying a spare engine. The newer AWACS also has a hard-point under the right wing, and there has been speculation that the E–3A might carry electronic countermeasure pods under the wings.

The E–3A can certainly take care of itself against most radar-directed missiles, although it is a tempting target, radiating huge amounts of power over five hundred miles. The pods would be a short-range defense only, probably against the infrared missiles of fighters that had sneaked through the escort. (The F–15s of Soesterberg are reported to have a major mission of AWACS and tanker escort.) The AWACS would be a prime candidate for a self-defense laser system of the type the USAF is currently testing on a modified EC–130, but until this bit of science fiction is realized, the AWACS will have to take fighters off the line to defend itself. In fact, the air battles of the next war might more closely resemble carrier battles in the Pacific during World War II, as AWACS from both sides vector fighters against each other, spoofing and jamming all the way.

The AWACS could also help out in one of the stickiest problems facing USAFE pilots in central Europe. It all has to do with a little gizmo called the IFF transponder. IFF stands for Identification Friend or Foe and allows aircraft and ground installations to distinguish between friendly and enemy aircraft. If it works, radar air-to-air missiles and SAMs can knock down enemy aircraft well beyond visual range. When it doesn't work, as was often the case in Vietnam and among the Arab forces in the 1973 Mideast war, friendlies can shoot down friendlies.

IFF is a big problem, but it has even larger ramifications. It has led to arguments about a lot of small, cheap fighters versus very capable, very expensive ones. It has spawned the development of a whole new generation of missiles. It has even changed the future of air combat.

Understanding this takes a little background. The first requirements for an air-to-air missile evolved from a need for a weapon that would counter the kamikaze attacks that raked American naval task forces in the later stages of the war in the Pacific. But the first practicable air-to-air missile wasn't developed until the mid-fifties, with the AIM–9 Sidewinder.

The Sidewinder was the first successful air-to-air missile, and the first passive infrared weapon to become operational with U.S. forces. The first kill ever attributed to an air-to-air missile occurred in 1958, when a Nationalist Chinese F–86 pilot shot down a Red Chinese MiG–17 with an AIM–9B. The Soviet Atoll began as a virtual copy of an early Sidewinder.

The radar-guided AIM–7 Sparrow was developed at about the same time. It is a semi-active radar-homing weapon, riding on the radar beam of its parent fighter until it gets close enough to complete the intercept under its own guidance.

The Sidewinder and the Sparrow have since been developed to such an extent that they are probably the most advanced air-to-air missiles currently in use. The latest version of the Sidewinder, the AIM–9L, has an off-boresight, all-aspect capability, which means it can be fired at virtually any quadrant of the target, and, thanks to the cooled infrared seeker head slaved to the radar, the firing plane doesn't have to be facing directly at the target—data from the radar give the missile a "head start" before it leaves the plane. (Fighter pilots never call the AIM-9L a Sidewinder, preferring the more operational-sounding "Nine" or "Lima." A Sidewinder is also referred to as a "Fox Two" in a system that delineates attack according to weapons and ranges—long-range missiles are called "Fox One"; short-range missiles, "Fox Two"; guns are called "Fox Three"; and "Fox Four," according to one USAFE pilot, is a midair collision.) The Sparrow has also been improved to the point where the latest versions, the AIM-7F2 and the AIM-7L, have *some* look-down, shoot-down capability.

But both missiles have their origins in 1950s technology and have shortcomings that became all too apparent in Southeast Asia. The Sidewinders there often tracked the sun or the earth, and although this is no longer such a problem with the AIM-9Ls, they are still subject to electronic countermeasures or outmaneuvering.

The Sparrow has similar problems but has an even bigger drawback: The firing pilot must still point his aircraft at the target for an uncomfortably long period of time to lock on to the target and provide the beam for the missile to home in on. So even though the attacker may have launched his Sparrow well beyond visual range, by the time it reaches the target, the enemy and the friendly plane are almost at each other's throats. If, for some reason, the Sparrow missed its target (quite possible, as in Southeast Asia both the AIM-9 and the AIM-7 had dismally low probabilities of kill), the attacker was forced into a dogfight with smaller, more agile planes, where its BVR (Beyond Visual Range) capability was useless, and it was forced to turn for its life. This happened quite often, especially in Vietnam, where IFF doubts and

rules of engagement meant the big F-4 interceptors had to visually acquire the smaller, more maneuverable MiGs before firing any missiles. Since, by definition, there can be no firing of BVR missiles in a situation where visual identification is required, the Phantom drivers in Vietnam often sent one member of the flight charging through the enemy formation, afterburners flaring, to radio back to his buddies whether to shoot or not to shoot. This was a less than optimum solution, and the development of better air-to-air missiles was a high post–Vietnam War priority.

The Air Force concentrated on a Sidewinder replacement. Their first attempt, the AIM-82A program to develop an all-aspect launch-and-leave missile for the new FX fighter, was canceled after two months.

The Navy came up with a very sophisticated vectored-thrust missile called AGILE, developed at the Naval Weapons Center at China Lake, California. (Many successful USAF programs started life as Navy projects—the F-4 and the A-7, for example—as well as most of their missiles, including the Sidewinder, Sparrow, Shrike, and Standard ARM. There's not much difference between the Air Force and Navy missiles, except, as one Wild Weasel pilot says, "We take them and change the designation and make them cost more." But what else can one expect from the USAF, whose standard 500-pound bomb weighs 580 pounds?)

The Air Force's answer to the AGILE was a rapid-fire, relatively cheap and light, infrared missile. The Air Force, always willing to walk the extra mile for a good acronym, called it the CLAW, or Concept of a Lightweight Aerial Weapon.

This was in 1975, when Congress no longer opened its checkbook to anyone in uniform. Already a bit miffed about lack of air-to-air missile commonality (some of the later Sidewinders will work on either USAF or Navy planes, but not both) and perplexed that both the Air Force and the Navy were embarking on two separate and expen-

Bitburg F-15 jocks debrief their "2 v. 2" contest with Alconbury aggressor pilot-instructors. Engagement is elaborately recreated on board with colored chalk.

ACEVAL tests. Originally a sort of fly-off between the Navy AGILE and the Air Force CLAW (this was the AIMVAL part, the Air Intercept Missile Evaluation), the tests were later expanded to include other aspects of air-to-air combat (Air Combat Evaluation, the ACEVAL section).

For the original tests, the "Blue Force" was comprised of six Air Force F-15s and six Navy F-14s. Fifteen Air Force F-5Es were tagged for the "Red Force" to simulate threat aircraft. The tests took part over the extensive Air Combat Maneuvering Range at Nellis AFB in Nevada.

AIMVAL-ACEVAL provided very valuable information to the services, as well as to the designers of the new missile prototypes, the Advanced Short Range Air-To-Air Missile (ASRAAM) Sidewinder replacement, and the Sparrow successor, the Advanced Medium Range Air-To-Air Missile (AMRAAM). But much of what has been printed and broadcast about the tests was distorted by the media, aided and abetted by various rival contractors. One prophetic official summed it up while the tests were still going on: "I'm afraid nobody is going to take the time to review the rules before coming to conclusions."

Here are some of those rules: The F-5s of the Red Team, simulating MiG-21s, were allowed to carry AIM-9L Sidewinders, the most advanced short-range missile in the USAF inventory. It's doubtful the Soviets have a missile nearly as capable, and by the time they get it, it won't be hung on a MiG-21. The Red Team was also directed by unrealistically precise ground control intercept units in unrealistically clear weather (one USAFE pilot says the best thing about flying in Nevada is that the nearest cloud is in Iowa).

The Blue Team, on the other hand, fought with one hand tied behind its back. The F-14s, in particular, were at a disadvantage. Virtually built around the ultra-long-range AIM-54 Phoenix missile, the Tomcats were not allowed to use them at AIMVAL-ACEVAL. And the F-5s often managed

sive programs to develop a weapon that would essentially do the same thing, Congress cut the CLAW and AGILE projects out of the budget and intimated that if the services needed such a program they would have to get together on it.

They got together at Nellis Air Force Base in September 1975 for the now-famous AIMVAL-

to hide themselves in the clutter of ground return by flying at ultra low levels—because it is a carrier plane, built for maritime use, the F–14's sophisticated radar was at a disadvantage over land.

The rules were biased in favor of the F–5s to present a "worst case" scenario, a credit to the original AIMVAL-ACEVAL program directors. After all, the whole point of the exercise was to see what could go wrong, not what the Air Force did right. But the results were twisted in the media, and the moral of the story, if we are to believe articles in the popular press, is that the United States ought to buy more F–5s!

"It causes a great deal of consternation, I think, in the government, when comparisons are drawn that maybe shouldn't be drawn in the first place," says a Bitburg Eagle pilot.

And I think it's fueled, to some extent, by the contractors. Nothing makes a contractor happier than to see some guy write an article about how X airplane defeated Y airplane in totally unrealistic conditions without using their real missiles and a lot of training constraints. I think most pilots, regardless of which airplane they flew in that encounter, would tend to blow it off as being bogus.

But the lesson burned into people's minds from reading published results of AIMVAL-ACEVAL goes something like this:

If both planes have to see each other to launch missiles, then both pilots will die, due to the modern infrared missile's ability to guide itself to the target even if its firing aircraft is destroyed. One pilot will die a fraction of a second before the other, but both will launch missiles and both will be killed. So why build big, expensive airplanes, like the F–14 and the F–15, when you're going to wind up trading one-for-one anyway? Why not just buy a bunch of cheap, less sophisticated planes like the F–16 and the F–5?

So what started out as an exercise to see how best to optimize the capability of America's most advanced fighters turned into a commercial for a giant step backward in aircraft design. Besides, America cannot bring itself to produce a cheap fighter, as evidenced by the F–16 program. They can build good, small fighters, but everything they touch turns into gold—for somebody. Supporters of the F–16 say it is just as good a dogfighter as the F–15—perhaps better, because it's much smaller (if AIMVAL-ACEVAL taught the USAF anything, it's that smaller is better in fighter design). It lacks the long range radar and Beyond Visual Range missiles of the F–15, but these would be useless in a visual environment, which they maintain is all you are likely to have in central Europe due to IFF problems.

This leads us back to IFF, the little gizmo that is causing all the problems. The first IFF (Identification Friend or Foe) system was operated by the Allies in World War II and was almost immediately compromised by the Germans. The Luftwaffe's FuG–25A IFF system was in turn broken and used against them by British night fighters intercepting bombers over England.

The current "standard" NATO IFF is the U.S. Mark XII system. Although it has been updated, the basic design is over twenty years old. Some analysts believe it is subject to jamming or even spoofing, allowing hostile aircraft to mimic friendlies or pass unhindered.

Although the details of encrypting and breaking IFF codes are technologically complicated, the basic premise of the system is pretty simple. A USAFE Phantom pilot explains:

IFF/SIF is very common—even 747s have it. SIF (Selective Identification Feature) is just to separate this guy from that guy. IFF is something a combat plane would have to make it unique from every other plane in the air. I may have a four digit code on my IFF/SIF, and a guy flying ten miles over there may have a four digit code that is different from mine so they can tell us apart on the radar. I really don't know how the thing works.

They just say "Squawk this on your IFF/SIF" and you spin in the numbers and it's all cosmic. There may be a particular code that's a secret between me and the ground radar station so they'll know not to shoot me, but they'll shoot anybody else that doesn't have that particular code.

But can't the IFF transponder be jammed?

Yeah, you can jam anything. But once again, there are stages of alert that you go to, passive and active modes. Something like that's hard to jam because you interrogate it, you aren't going to be transmitting all the time. You'd have to have a tremendous power to jam something like that.

But even though it's difficult to jam IFF, it's not impossible, and the Soviets are believed to have made IFF-jamming a high priority. One of the biggest drawbacks of the current system is that it works perfectly well in peacetime and might lull NATO planners into a false sense of security. Even if the system isn't jammed or spoofed, it is subject to saturation. And the nature of IFF means that if it is compromised just once, it poisons the whole system and degrades its effectiveness to a tremendous degree. The whole point of jamming or tricking IFF is not to cause friendlies to shoot

RF-4C recon Phantom is rolled into Alconbury hangar for quick film reload. Photos just shot will be available for viewing in under an hour.

down friendlies—the point is to introduce enough doubt into the system to require positive visual identification of targets before firing, and many analysts believe the Soviets have that capability.

Naturally, USAFE planners recognize the danger and have taken steps to counter it. They are extremely close-mouthed about their Airspace Control Plan, as well they should be, but it is believed to carve up central Europe into Safe Haven Areas and altitude bands and free-fire zones. It is a well thought out system, but how smoothly it would work in wartime is anybody's guess. It is interesting to note that in some NATO exercises, as much as 40 percent of the "losses" were reportedly due to friendly fire.

If it's any consolation, the Soviets apparently have yet to solve the difficult problems of operating fighters and ground-based defenses in the same airspace. SAMs from the same battery that shot down Francis Gary Powers's U-2 also re-

RF-4C has film pulled from its multiple cameras at RAF Alconbury. Recon calls for guts: first in, last out, and no armament.

portedly downed some of the MiGs that were chasing him. This incident was repeated many times in Vietnam. The Soviet IFF system was severely compromised when Lieutenant Viktor Belenko defected to the West and analysts pored over the Soviet "ODD-RODS" system carried in his MiG-25.

The Soviets solve some of the problem by assigning most of the defense of the battlefield to ground-based systems. But in any war the lines would soon be blurred, and it's doubtful air defense can be so neatly compartmentalized. Still, it seems the Soviets are willing to take their chances on IFF.

"They have a much different philosophy," says one USAFE pilot.

In a regular army you lay down artillery, then you lift the barrage and your guys go for it. But they found that if they just kept blasting artillery in there on top of their own guys they'd lose less people. Would we do that? Of course not. We'd lose more people, but we wouldn't kill any of our own.

IFF is a much bigger problem for NATO. After all, at least every Warsaw Pact nation uses the same IFF system. And NATO fighters are, on the whole, more capable at Beyond Visual Range fighting than the point-defense MiG-21s that provide the bulk of the Warsaw Pact nations' fighter inventories.

There is no real standardized IFF system for NATO. As usual, everybody wants everybody else

to conform to one system as long as it's theirs. The first attempt to develop a truly integrated NATO IFF system was stifled in 1981, when Congress cut 90 percent of the proposed funding from a development program.

No one disputes that NATO IFF is a problem. But just how big a problem it is seems to depend on where you're sitting. High-ranking commanders and ground-based radar and SAM operators seem to think the Airspace Control Plan will work smoothly. But fighter pilots have a different view. Uncharacteristically, they refuse to talk about it on the record. Off the record they are scared to death.

IFF discrimination could be the AWACS' biggest contribution in the central European theater. Half of its huge rotodome is devoted to IFF antennae. The E-3A's radar could conceivably keep tabs on

E-3A AWACS, skunk-striped rotodome turning lazily, loiters at 40,000 feet over eastern Belgium. AWACS flights often extend beyond 12 hours with double flight crews.

Warsaw Pact aircraft from the moment they take off all the way to interception, however low they fly. It can certainly do the same for Western aircraft, no matter what kind of IFF they carry. It could be that IFF problems were the whole rationale for building a control center in an AWACS in the first place, rather than have the airplane be just a flying radar antenna relaying messages to a ground control center, which is how the Europeans first envisioned the AWACS. If it can begin to solve NATO's IFF problems, the prodigiously expensive E-3A AWACS may turn out to be a multimillion-dollar bargain.

Chapter 6
USAFE: Brickyard Blues

In some parts of USAFE, Ramstein is called The Brickyard in that peculiar tone of awe and contempt usually reserved for institutions, like the Internal Revenue Service, that can be ridiculed but never ignored. The term *Brickyard* does not come from goldbricking as might first be imagined—there is a certain amount of goldbricking performed at USAFE headquarters to be sure, but that is a World War II term and military slang goes out of fashion more rapidly than jazz lingo. The "brick" in Brickyard refers instead to the small Motorola walkie-talkies carried by the Ramstein brass. The black wire-whipped bricks are the ultimate fashion statement for high-ranking officers.

And there are enough high-ranking officers at Ramstein to keep enlisted men saluting themselves silly. Veterans of the U.S. Army, who might have spent their entire military careers without ever coming into contact with anyone above the rank of captain, are constantly amazed by the parade of oak leaves, eagles, and stars on the Ramstein epaulets.

It is quite a sight, this gathering of eagles. They flock at the O-Club. They formate at the endless Ramstein ceremonies; the majors, colonels, even generals, all uniformly casual, all rigidly at ease, their feet spread, their hands clasped behind them

as if they were a gang of thieves about to be led away to the paddy wagon.

And always the brick, the transistorized scepter of power, the digital swagger stick is clutched in the officer's hand, squeezing out messages that are rarely for him.

Brickmanship is not limited to officers. Sometimes a particularly indispensable enlisted specialist will get his own solid-state status symbol, but this is just gravy. For a full colonel, however, a brick is an absolute necessity, and to be without one would be as humiliating as being vice-president of the firm and not being carboned. Sometimes, if he is pulling double duty—a staff officer, for example, serving a temporary stint as supervisor of flying—or if he is simply a flaming overachiever, an officer will carry *two* bricks, but even in Ramstein this is looked upon as a bit much.

At the other end of the portable radio arms race —and Ramstein is one of the few places on earth where this phenomenon can be observed—an officer can attain a rank so exalted he no longer needs to carry a brick. This doesn't mean he doesn't have one (perish the thought!). It just means he no longer needs to lug it around himself. An aide, following a respectful three steps behind our general, carries it for him.

Ramstein is a Mecca for high-ranking commanders simply because there is so much to command. The USAFE figures are staggering: 57,000 command military personnel; 24,000 from other major air commands, Military Airlift Command and Strategic Air Command contributing the most; 16,000 American and Local workers; and almost 93,000 family members. USAFE maintains a presence in almost every NATO country from Iceland to Greece, and its area of responsibility extends out through the Mediterranean to North Africa, the Middle East, and the Persian Gulf. There are more than 700 of the most advanced, expensive, and lethal airplanes ever built in the current USAFE inventory.

To keep track of all this, USAFE has worked out a chain of command that looks deceptively simple. USAFE reports to the U.S. Air Force and to USEUCOM, a unified command that exercises operational control over all American Army, Navy, Air Force, and Marine units in Europe through its headquarters in Stuttgart-Vaihingen, West Germany.

USAFE commands its units through three numbered air forces: the 3rd Air Force, headquartered at RAF Mildenhall in England; the 16th Air Force, headquartered at Torrejón Air Base in Spain; and the 17th Air Force, headquartered at Sembach Air Base in West Germany.

That's the way it works on paper, but in reality the USAFE command structure is much more subtle. For instance, in 1976, under a project called Creek Swap, the commander of Ramstein's resident tactical fighter wing, the 86th TFW, became host commander for the Kaiserslautern Military Community, major domo to the 50,000 Air Force and Army personnel and dependents who live and work at Ramstein, Landstuhl, Army Kasernes and Sembach Air Base. Since the Kaiserslautern Military Community is the largest single community of Americans overseas, it took up a lot of the 86th TFW commander's time, so a new organization, the 86th Tactical Fighter Group, was created to oversee the operations of the wing's two Phantom squadrons, the 512th and the 526th TFS. The squadron commanders report to the 86th TFG commander, who reports to the 86th TFW commander, who reports, theoretically at least, to the commander of the 17th Air Force at Sembach Air Base. Sembach Air Base, meanwhile, is part of the Kaiserslautern Military Community, the head of which is . . . the 86th Tactical Fighter Wing commander! So the two men are, on paper, each other's bosses! (Wonderful! Have to have lunch sometime. Don't squawk me, I'll squawk you.)

Actually, the USAFE chain of command is not as bizarre as this example, admittedly taken out of context, would suggest. But it is complex. Ramstein is a dynamic place because USAFE is a dynamic command, with units from everywhere going every which way under different states of duty—TDY, rotational, and permanently assigned —and under various degrees of USAFE command. Keeping track of all this, especially during the seemingly ceaseless USAFE exercises, keeps Ramstein's bricks barking and screeching.

One wonders how USAFE got along before the invention of the portable radio. Well, things were simpler in the beginning. Way back in 1945, when USAFE was first put together from elements of the old wartime United States Strategic Air Forces in Europe, USAFE was more interested in getting rid of weapons than using them. Its first mission was disposing of huge amounts of U.S. and Luftwaffe war material. As this mission was completed, most of its personnel were transferred or demobilized, and by 1947 USAFE became a predominately administrative command, headquartered in Saint-Germain-en-Laye, France.

Things didn't stay quiet for long. On the night of June 23, 1948, the Soviet Union, alleging a coal shortage, cut off electrical power to West Berlin. Railroads and highways around the city were soon blocked, and West Berlin found itself cut off from the West.

The allies answered with Operation Vittles. Elements of USAFE, along with units from the RAF and other Western allies, participated in the Berlin airlift, flying 100,000 tons of supplies aboard 20,000 flights into West Berlin in the first month alone.

The blockade was lifted eleven months later, but Operation Vittles continued until September, 1949. Stirred into action by the blockade and the subsequent dashing of any hopes for a perpetually peaceful Europe, the nations of Western Europe formed the North Atlantic Treaty Organization in April of that year. USAFE had acquired a new life during the airlift, and with the formation of NATO, the need and nature of the command's military role became clear. USAFE began to build up.

NATO forces in West Germany were originally deployed along the lines of the old Allied zones of occupation, which were themselves assigned according to such vagaries as who landed where on D-Day. So, paradoxically, the most easily defended territory, the rugged terrain of central Germany, is protected by the powerful forces of the United States. And the flat, barren plains of northern Germany—including the Luneberg Heath, perfect country for the Soviet style of massive mechanized assault—is defended by the United Kingdom, whose economic difficulties and political whirlpool in Northern Ireland are draining the strength from the proud but weakened British Army of the Rhine.

USAFE's deployment was improved in 1951, when the French government granted the Americans the right to construct bases in France and in the French Occupational Zone of Germany. When France withdrew from NATO over doubts about the United States' willingness to risk an all-out nuclear war to save Europe, the French government ordered the removal of all foreign military forces by April 1, 1967. Nine major bases and seventy-eight other USAFE installations in France were shut down, their assets transferred to other parts of the command. But USAFE retained some of the key bases in the old French Occupational Zone of Germany, and these bases in the Eifel provide the backbone of the 17th Air Force today.

With the expulsion from France, USAFE headquarters was moved to Wiesbaden, near the huge West German industrial center of Frankfurt am Main. In 1973, the headquarters moved again, to its present location at Ramstein, seven miles west of Kaiserslautern and thirty miles east of the French border. Ramstein's 3,000 acres make it the largest U.S. air base in Europe.

It is also the busiest. Ramstein is not only the site of USAFE headquarters and the 86th Tactical Fighter Wing, it is also the headquarters of Allied Air Forces Central Europe (AAFCE). Both the Strategic Air Command and the Military Airlift Command exercise control over their units in Europe through headquarters at Ramstein. In addition, the Brickyard houses a swarm of other specialized organizations, ranging from the 7055th Operations Squadron, which makes sure units from other NATO nations can deliver U.S. nuclear weapons, to the less apocalyptic 686th Air Force Band.

Ramstein gets even busier during the frequent European exercises, especially REFORGER (Redeployment of Forces to Germany). Held every year in the early fall, REFORGER integrates units from every branch of the American armed forces in the West's most extensive war games. USAFE's operational contribution to the REFORGER exercises is called Cold Fire; the deployment of U.S.-based air assets to Europe is called Crested Cap.

The 4th Tactical Fighter Wing of Seymour Johnson Air Force Base, North Carolina, is "dual-based" at Ramstein. One or two of the 4th's squadrons return to the Brickyard every year for Crested Cap, like swallows to Capistrano. But most Crested Cap units are regular Tactical Air Command (TAC) line squadrons—the purpose is to see how quickly air reinforcements can be assimilated into the central European environment.

USAFE's tactical aircraft are roughly divided as to mission as well as geographic boundaries, with the 17th Air Force in Germany well stocked with fighters, and the 3rd Air Force in England flying predominately strike and close air support aircraft.

The 16th Air Force is the smallest air force in USAFE, with only one fighter wing, the 401st TFW, based at Torrejón, Spain. The wing's squadrons, the 612th, 613th, and 614th TFS, each have a strength of eighteen F-4Ds, six aircraft less than comparable USAFE fighter squadrons. The 16th Air Force's other main unit, the 406th Tactical Fighter Training Wing at Zaragoza, has no aircraft permanently assigned to it. The 406th acts as a "holding wing" for rotational units and supports USAFE aircraft on training deployments. The wing is also responsible for the operation and maintenance of USAFE ranges in Spain.

The 16th Air Force doesn't get much publicity, but it is a vital part of the USAFE structure. Its wide-open weapons ranges are a particularly valuable asset in the otherwise crowded European environment. And the 16th controls a number of important standby bases throughout the southern Mediterranean. Duty in the 16th is popular with USAFE aircrews, who often look back upon their days in Spain with pleasant memories.

In contrast to the 16th Air Force, the 3rd Air Force in England is a crowded, active command, with over 350 aircraft and seven active bases. Not only is the 3rd Air Force the oldest numbered air force in USAFE (it was activated in 1951, the 17th was activated in 1953, the 16th in 1966), it can trace its history in England back to 1942. The old 3rd Air Force trained and equipped units of the 8th Air Force, "The Mighty Eighth" that carried the war to Nazi Germany from airfields in East Anglia. Many current 3rd Air Force units also took part in that air war over Europe.

The modern 3rd Air Force began as the 3rd Air Division (Provisional) in 1948, at RAF Marham, Norfolk. In its inaugural year, the B-29s of the Air Division's three Bombardment Groups, based at RAF stations in Norfolk, Lincolnshire, and Suffolk, took part in the Berlin Airlift. The 3rd Air Division headquarters was moved to Bushy Park, then South Ruislip, both in Middlesex. In 1972, the headquarters of what was now known as the 3rd Air Force moved to its current location at RAF Mildenhall, Suffolk.

A favorite haunt for hordes of British tail spotters is RAF Alconbury, Cambridgeshire. An old 8th Air Force B-24 and B-17 base, Alconbury is now the home of the 10th Tactical Reconnaissance Wing. The 10th is unique in two respects: First, it is comprised of only two squadrons, the 1st Tactical Reconnaissance Squadron (TRS) and the 527th Tactical Fighter Training Aggressor Squadron (TFTAS); second, the two squadrons have completely different aircraft and missions.

The 1st TRS flies RF-4Cs; its mission is battlefield reconnaissance. The 527th TFTAS is an "Aggressor Squadron" and provides Dissimilar Air Combat Training (DACT) to USAFE pilots, flying Soviet tactics with their specially camouflaged F-5Es. When the 527th was first established at Alconbury in 1976, tail spotters had a field day as aircraft from all over USAFE came to the base to take on the Aggressors. But since the 36th Tactical Fighter Wing in Bitburg converted to F-15s a year later, some of their Eagles have been almost permanently deployed at Alconbury, and the 527th has taken to the road to provide DACT to USAFE aircrews.

RAF Alconbury recently welcomed another unique unit, the 17th Reconnaissance Wing. The wing's sole squadron, the 95th Reconnaissance Squadron, flies high-altitude recce missions with its TR-1 aircraft, an updated version of the old U-2 "Useless Deuce." Although it remains a SAC unit, the 17th reports directly to USAFE in peacetime and in wartime will become a NATO asset. The 81st Tactical Fighter Wing, which is stationed at the "twin" bases of RAF Bentwaters and RAF Woodbridge, Suffolk, has no less than six tactical fighter squadrons, the 78th, 91st, 92nd, 509th, 510th, and 511th, all flying the A-10 Thunderbolt II close air support aircraft. Although the bases are five miles apart, they are linked by a long taxiway. The 81st, which maintains its headquarters at Bentwaters, operates from both of these bases.

The airspace over Bentwaters/Woodbridge is not as crowded as might first be imagined, however, since at any given time a large part of the 81st TFW is deployed. The 81st maintains four Forward Operating Locations (FOL) in Germany and at least one-third of the wing is always deployed at their FOL. Each detachment consists of about a hundred men and eight aircraft. Det 1's FOL is Sembach Air Base, a USAFE airfield. The other FOLs are West German bases: Det 2 is at Leipheim, Det 3 is at Ahlhorn, and Det 4 is at Norvenich. Squadrons are usually assigned to the same detachments, the 510th to Det 1, the 92nd to Det 2, the 91st to Det 3, and the 78th to Det 4. The 511th is usually assigned to either Det 1 or 2, the 509th to 3 or 4.

Even more numerous in the 3rd Air Force inventory than A-10s are the F-111 strike aircraft, although these are divided between two bases. The 20th TFW at RAF Upper Heyford, Oxfordshire, operates three squadrons, the 55th, 77th, and 79th TFS, all equipped with F-111Es. The 48th TFW at RAF Lakenheath, Suffolk, operates the more powerful F-111Fs and consists of four squadrons, the 492nd, 493rd, 494th, and 495th TFS. The two bases are by no means "twins" however—RAF Upper Heyford, which can trace its history back to World War I when it was used as an RAF training base, is west of London, about twenty miles north of Oxford. RAF Lakenheath is in East Anglia, not far from RAF Mildenhall, and close to Oxford's rival, Cambridge. RAF Upper Heyford is also scheduled to receive the new RF-111A electronic countermeasure aircraft in the near future.

Unlike the 3rd Air Force, which has no dedicated air defense units, the 17th Air Force in Germany is loaded with fighters. Perhaps the most famous unit in USAFE—certainly the most photographed and written-about—is the 36th TFW at Bitburg, in the Eifel. The wing consists of three squadrons, the 22nd, the 53rd, and the 525th TFS. The 36th is used to publicity, having been the first European unit to receive the F-84, F-86, F-100, F-105, and in 1977, the F-15 Eagle.

The only other unit in USAFE equipped with F-15s is the 32nd TFS, stationed at Camp New Amsterdam located at the Dutch base of Soesterberg, in the Netherlands. The 32nd is also the only USAFE unit that reports directly to another nation —Holland—for operational control.

Spangdahlem is just over the hill from Bitburg, near the famous wine country of the Mosel valley and Trier, Germany's oldest city. In fact, Spangdahlem is so close to Bitburg the 36th TFW used to operate Spangdahlem as a satellite base to relieve congestion at Bitburg. But in 1972 one of the 36th's old squadrons, the 23rd TFS, took up permanent residence at Spangdahlem and became the nucleus of the base's current parent unit, the 52nd TFW.

Besides the F-4D-equipped 23rd TFS, the wing consists of the 480th TFS, flying F-4Es, and the 81st TFS, which operates the new F-4G "Wild Weasel" electronic warfare aircraft, the latest and probably last variant of the venerable Phantom. USAFE plans to eventually station another F-15 unit in Europe and Spangdahlem appears to be the likely site.

Until a short while ago, the 50th Tactical Fighter Wing at Hahn, in the German Hünsruck, operated the F-4 as well, with its three squadrons, the 10th, 313th, and 525th TFS, all equipped with F-4Es. But the 50th has just converted to the new F-16 Fighting Falcon. The Hahn F-16s are the latest "Block 16" aircraft, with the new, enlarged tailplane that facilitates takeoffs with heavier bomb loads. Ironically enough, even though the 50th is the first American overseas unit to fly the F–16, they are not the first F–16-equipped unit in Europe. That honor goes to the Belgian 349th Escadrille at Beauvechain, who have been zipping around in the Electric Jet since 1979. Two other USAFE tactical fighter wings are also scheduled to convert to the F–16: the 401st TFW at Torrejón in 1983 and the 86th TFW at Ramstein in 1986.

One other USAFE squadron flies Phantoms, the 26th TRW at Zweibrücken, an ex-Canadian base near the large southwestern German city of Saarbrücken. The 20th has shrunk in recent years, due partly to the USAFE's emphasis on using reconnaissance drones for dangerous battlefield work. The wing's sole remaining squadron, the 38th TRS, operates twenty RF–4Cs.

One of the most important but least publicized USAFE bases in Germany, Sembach Air Base is not only the headquarters of the 17th Air Force and a Forward Operating Location of A–10 aircraft, but also houses an Allied Tactical Operations Center and the USAFE Air Ground Operations School.

But Sembach's main tenant is the 601st Tactical Control Wing. The 601st is responsible for controlling air operations in central Europe through an extensive network of mobile radars and a tactical air support system of airborne and ground-based forward air controllers.

The 601st is the largest wing in USAFE, with half of its six thousand personnel scattered out in fifty-six different locations from the North Sea to northern Italy. Many of them are colocated with Army units and go out on field exercises with the grunts, calling in mock air strikes from communications jeeps. Although the 601st is headquartered at Sembach, it also maintains a sizable presence at Hessisch-Oldendorf Air Station in northern Germany, near Hannover, with the 600th Tactical Control Group.

The 601st's flying elements consist of the 20th and the 704th Tactical Air Support Squadrons, each operating about twenty OV–10 forward air control aircraft. The third flying squadron is the 601st Tactical Air Support Squadron, which uses its six CH–53 helicopters to support the operations of the 601st's mobile radar units.

The last USAFE tactical unit doesn't get much publicity either, but that's the way they like it. The 7th Special Operations Squadron operates out of Rhein-Main airport in Frankfurt, flying four MC–130 Combat Talon aircraft. Their mission is to carry USAF Combat Control Teams, Navy SEALS (underwater demolition experts), or Army Special Forces units in and out of enemy territory.

The Combat Talon is a very special version of the workhorse Hercules, with sophisticated electronic countermeasure and navigational gear. The aircraft's most distinguishable feature is the retractable Y-shaped nose yoke, used in the Fulton recovery system. Designed by the great-great-grandson of the inventor of the steamboat, the Fulton STAR (Surface To Air Recovery) literally snatches people from danger on the ground; the passenger dons a special harness and inflates a couple of helium balloons that tow a lifeline high enough to snag the low-flying plane. He is then winched aboard the aircraft. To make this even more dangerous, most of the 7th's routine training missions are done at night at very low altitudes.

Although this completes the list of USAFE tactical units and active bases, it is only part of the USAF's commitment to Europe (see the Appendix, "Support to USAFE"). Since 1945, four years before the formation of NATO and ten years before the signing of the Warsaw Pact, the United States Air Forces in Europe have been helping to protect the skies of Germany, our old enemy and modern ally, against aggression from our former friend and current rival, the Soviet Union. It is a big job, but—contrary to popular American belief—USAFE gets a great deal of help from the NATO allies, as we shall see in the next chapter.

Chapter 7
NATO: Mutual Support

Let's play the NATO numbers game!

Anyone can play: ill-informed politicians, parochial patriots, guileful contractors, self-appointed "defense experts" in the media, and all manner of professional analysts who should know better and often do. All it takes is the most elementary knowledge of central European military statistics and something to prove. Soon you too can conjure up the ominous tread of the Russian War Machine or sing a gentle lullaby of Soviet awkwardness and obsolescence. It's easy! It's fun! Let's go!

"In central Europe, NATO aircraft are outnumbered by the Soviets' three to one," say the pessimists. "The Russians are developing many new aircraft that are equal or superior to many produced in the West. The Warsaw Pact's standardized equipment and authoritarian command structure make it more adaptable and flexible than NATO, whose hodgepodge of aging aircraft and national rivalries make command integration a nightmare. While NATO members balk at spending pennies for defense, the Soviet Union pours billions into an air arm rapidly growing in quantity and quality."

Or . . .

"The numbers of aircraft in the NATO and Warsaw Pact inventories are roughly equal," say the optimists. "Most NATO aircraft are superior to any produced in the East. The Warsaw Pact's standardized equipment and authoritarian command

structure make it much more rigid and inflexible than NATO, whose wide variety of equipment and tactics make it highly adaptive and unpredictable. With their great technological lead, the Western nations need only to maintain their present level of defense while the Soviet Union must spend billions in a futile attempt to catch up."

Sound familiar? As Mark Twain said, there are three kinds of lies: lies, damned lies, and statistics. With just the smallest amount of "hard" data, a clever analyst can make the numbers march across the computer screen and dance to his tune. But what's the real story?

It should be a simple matter to determine the inventory of the opposing forces in central Europe, but it is not. Oddly enough, the Soviets are not the problem; through satellite reconnaissance and conventional intelligence and by their own admission in treaty negotiations, we can get a rough but fairly accurate picture of the number of combat aircraft that could be fielded by the Soviet Union and the Warsaw Pact nations in a wartime situation.

It's the NATO allies that give the statisticians room to fudge the figures. The pessimistic three-to-one ratio heard so often does not take into account several important NATO air assets. And the wildly optimistic one-to-one figure includes

Flight of RAF Jaguar attack aircraft over southern England. French forces also operate Jaguars. *Photo: British Aircraft Corporation Ltd.*

many "best case" estimates not likely to be fully realized.

For example, there are the more than 1,500 American air reinforcements stationed in the United States but earmarked for deployment to Europe during wartime under the Crested Cap program. Or the two American carrier task forces that routinely prowl the Mediterranean. Or the other Marine and Naval air reinforcements operating on NATO's flanks, freeing up aircraft in the central region. Or even the large and formidable *Armée de l'Air.* (Although the French have long ago resigned from the formal NATO structure, they still exercise and communicate with allied forces. The French air force maintains a low-key presence at Ramstein, and it would be difficult to construct any central European war scenario in which France would not fight alongside NATO, at least in self-defense.)

Since there's no way to tell exactly how many of these reinforcements would get to central Europe, or what they would do when they got there, the Crested Cap, Marine, Navy, and French aircraft are often left out or put into the NATO inventory by analysts with particular axes to grind.

But even the precise numbers wouldn't tell the whole story. Also important in the military balance are the *types* of aircraft, that is, the kinds of missions they're capable of performing and their level of sophistication. Even though the West has consistently been outnumbered in the central region, it has always enjoyed a qualitative superiority, plane for plane. It still does. Thanks mainly to two wings of vital but still underappreciated F-111s in England, NATO can carry more ordnance farther and in worse weather than their Eastern rivals. And the Russians have yet to come up with anything to match the new F-15 and F-16 fighters now deployed in Europe.

But this could change. The Soviet Union is rapidly producing new, all-weather strike aircraft—the Su-24 Fencer, for example—and is developing a batch of more potent types. The West, on the other hand, is not cutting metal on any new designs. In fact, the NATO countries are having enough trouble putting aircraft already developed into operational service. The German-British-Italian Panavia Tornado started life at about the same time as the F-15 but has had an extraordinarily long teething program (raise your hand if you can remember when it was called the MRCA '75 Panther), and has still to see operational deployment. Likewise, the Luftwaffe version of the Alpha Jet trainer and close air support aircraft is still not in the hands of line pilots.

Collaboration is Western Europe's only hope to break the American monopoly on the Free World's combat aircraft market. But collaboration breeds delay as the different national partners jockey to build an aircraft closer to their requirements, often at the expense of the other members' needs. And delay means inflation eats up national budgets, so the partners wind up with fewer aircraft than they bargained for. Or they defer the program even further into the future, until what was once the hottest and most advanced combat aircraft in the world turns into a mere curiosity, produced in small numbers and compromised into ineffectuality.

Even now, the Tornado is slated to perform close air support, battlefield interdiction, counter-air ops, naval attack, air-superiority, interception, and reconnaissance missions. Although there will be slightly different variants for different roles, the basic airframe will remain the same. This sounds suspiciously like the disastrous Air Force–Navy TFX program, America's only experience with "collaboration" and, according to a somewhat biased F-111 driver at Lakenheath, on that golden day line pilots receive their Tornadoes, they will get an aircraft that is "smaller, not quite as fast, doesn't go as far, doesn't carry as much, and costs twice as much" as the F-111F.

Even in a low-risk collaborative program there are pitfalls. One of the first international projects, the SEPECAT Jaguar, was successful mainly because the English bullied the French into taking what was good for them. But the French still had to enter into another collaboration—this time with Germany and Belgium—to get the Alpha Jet, the trainer they had wanted from the Jaguar program in the first place.

Although the other partners have been flying the Alpha Jet for some time, the German variant developed engine and ejection problems at the last minute. The Luftwaffe really needed the Alpha Jet. The aircraft it replaced, the Fiat (Aeritalia) G.91, was over twenty years old (raise your hand if you remember when the A-4 Skyhawk was considered as an *interim* G.91 replacement in the late 1960s). The Gina won a NATO contest for a light tactical aircraft back in 1956 against a pair of eminently forgettable French aircraft, but true to the NATO spirit of cooperation and collaboration, it was adopted only by Italy, the manufacturer, and Germany, which didn't have much choice.

The need for a new air-superiority aircraft has led Germany to embark on another collaboration, this time with England and France. Between them, Europe's three largest nations should be able to come up with a pretty good airplane, but again the program is threatened, literally before it gets off the ground, by the conflicting needs of the partners.

France wants a ground attack aircraft, a Jaguar replacement. Britain at first wanted an aircraft to replace both the Jaguar and Harrier, but has now settled on just a Jaguar replacement. The real problem is Germany—the Luftwaffe needs a fighter. France has the new Mirage 2000, an advanced-technology version of its familiar delta-wing fighter series, as well as the more powerful private-venture Mirage 4000. Britain is pinning its air defense hopes on the Tornado ADV (Air Defense Variant).

At first this would seem another uncooperative European cooperative, but they may pull it off this time. After all, if it sounds like what they're looking for is an F-16, you're partly correct; what they're really looking for is a 1980s advanced-technology European version of the F-16. It's significant that each of the potential partners has released provisional designs that are remarkably similar, a twin-finned delta and canard. In fact, all the prototypes resemble the wreckage of a midair collision between a Mirage 2000, an F-16, and an F-18.

But the partners are already starting to drift apart. Germany, the odd man out as far as the primary mission is concerned and already strapped by defense spending and Tornado delays, seems to be cooling on the project. Italy, who never really was in, appears to be firmly out, with no mention of what will happen on that coming day when all of their Starfighters disintegrate in the sky from old age. (One last time: Raise your hand if you remember the Lockheed-Aeritalia *Lancer.* I thought so.) The French can, and probably will, take care of themselves. Meanwhile the British have announced plans to continue flying their Jaguars into the nineties.

It seems strange that NATO, which has such a clear-cut chain of command and whose nations work so well together in simulated wartime exercises, has no plans for peace. They have a very well thought out operation for making war, but no cohesive mechanism for making weapons. It is rather like the United Nations, where everything goes smoothly until someone decides his national interests—or more specifically, his national economic interests—are being threatened.

But the NATO nations do fly well together. Although USAFE is probably the most powerful air force in NATO, it is certainly not the only one. The British RAF, the modern West German *Luft-waffe,* the Belgian FAeB, the Dutch KLu, the Canadian RCAF, and the Danish KDF patrol the central European skies, performing the same missions as USAFE and—according to American pilots—performing them well.

"At our first exercise they threw guys from six countries together and the mission went like clockwork," says an F–4 backseater at Spangdahlem. "The guys over here really know what they're doing."

Professionalism is the norm in NATO. They may speak different languages and fly different airplanes, but a fighter pilot is a fighter pilot, whether he's a Dutch F–104 jock, a German F–4 driver, or an American Eagle pilot. The language problem isn't really much of a problem either—English is the international language of aviation, and many European pilots speak English more clearly than Americans do.

There's certainly no language barrier with British pilots. RAF Germany forms the backbone of NATO's Second Allied Tactical Air Force. RAFG's headquarters at Rheindahlem, near Mönchengladbach, is colocated with the headquarters of 2 ATAF (Second Allied Tactical Air Force), along with the headquarters of the Northern Army Group (NORTHAG) and that of the British Army of the Rhine. Two ATAF also maintains a wartime headquarters across the border at Maastricht, Holland. The commander of RAF Germany is also the Commander in Chief of 2 ATAF, directing German, Belgian, and Dutch air assets under his command.

Two ATAF's area of responsibility is all of Germany north of a line from Bonn to Kassel and out to the East German border, corresponding with the boundary between NORTHAG and CENTAG (Central Army Group). South of the line is 4 ATAF, headquartered at Heidelberg, under the command of a Luftwaffe lieutenant general. Almost all USAFE aircraft are committed to 4 ATAF, along with Luftwaffe and Canadian units, but Allied Air Forces Central Europe (AAFCE), whose commander is also the head of USAFE, has control of all NATO air assets in the central region. AAFCE was created in the 1974 reorganization plan to more smoothly effect the transition of the 1,500 aircraft of six nations from national command in peacetime to NATO command in wartime.

Although its military has suffered at the hands of Britain's floundering economy, the Royal Air Force's commitment to Germany is a promise they intend to keep. The once far-flung RAF has contracted its operations primarily to its home country and Germany. Like their counterparts in the British Army of the Rhine, the aircrews and personnel of RAF Germany are dedicated professionals, making the most of their rapidly aging equipment. The high cost of aviation fuel has caused most NATO nations to cut back on their flying hours, but it has hit the RAFG particularly hard. Nonessential flights are rare, and British participation in air shows has slackened off quite a bit in recent years.

Although the aircraft are flown to the edges of their envelopes—and more than occasionally beyond—the Phantoms, Buccaneers, Jaguars, and Harriers of the RAFG are being left behind in the technological arms race between the East and West. This is especially true in central Europe, where new types from both sides are currently being deployed.

The Buccaneer is twenty years old and scheduled to be replaced by the Tornado GR.1 next year, but as previously mentioned, the Tornado's entry into service has been delayed and is long overdue. The Harrier first flew in 1966, but the basic airframe design, the P.1127, is six years older. The American AV–8B Harrier derivative is now slated to supplement the existing RAF Harrier force, but if the latest European collaboration deal is as dead as it looks, there will be no solid replacement for the Jaguar. Although it is a sound design, the Jaguar never was what one would call the leading edge of technology, and even with new electronic countermeasures gear and uprated engines, it will be hard pressed to keep up.

RAFG operates from four bases in northern Germany: RAF Wildenrath and RAF Bruggen are on the West Germany–Netherlands border, south-west of the sprawling industrial cities of the Ruhr valley. RAF Laarbruch is farther north, next to Hopsten and at the edge of the Reichswald forest, scene of epic World War II battles at the end of the Nazi Siegfried Line during the winter of 1944/1945. RAF Gütersloh, the only RAFG base east of the Rhine, is near Bielefeld, headquarters of 1st (British) Corps, BAOR.

The RAFG's fighter force is based at Wildenrath, with No. 19 and No. 92 squadrons flying Phantom FGR.2s. The British Phantoms have Rolls-Royce Spey engines and no internal cannon, although they routinely carry the M-61 Vulcan gun pod. Other armament includes the Sky Flash, a radar missile similar to the American AIM-7M Sparrow, and the AIM-9G Sidewinder. A new program, called SEAM, for Sidewinder Expanded Acquisition Mode, will enable the FGR.2s to use the more advanced AIM-9L, giving them an off-boresight, all-aspect capability. The Wildenrath Phantoms are dedicated air-defense aircraft and are currently undergoing a gradual metamorphosis from their old gray and green camouflage to the new matte gray finish favored for modern air-superiority fighters.

Just north of Wildenrath, Bruggen houses four squadrons, No. 14, No. 17, No. 20, and No. 31, all equipped with Jaguars. Like most RAFG bases, Bruggen has recently been given the new "toned-down" look. Buildings and vehicles were painted a drab green to match the surrounding woods. Even the runways were chemically treated to camouflage them from the air. The hardened aircraft shelters were constructed so no two face exactly the same direction; any bomb that damages one shelter would not necessarily damage another. The whole effect is boring but businesslike and makes the base seem much smaller than it actually is.

There is also a single Jaguar unit at Laarbruch—No. 2 (AC) squadron, charged with deep reconnaissance missions—but the base is primarily a roost for the Buccaneer S.2Bs of No. XV and 16 squadrons. Their mission is similar to that of the USAFE F-111s in England: counter-air, nuclear strike, and conventional long-range interdiction. There are also four Hunter T.7 trainers at Laarbruch. Attached to No. XV Squadron, the Hunters were used to keep Buccaneer pilots current while their aging aircraft were grounded following an accident at Red Flag '80. The trainers are now used in the "aggressor" role.

Gütersloh is the home of RAFG's Harriers, the amazing vertical takeoff and landing aircraft. The Harrier GR.3s and two-place T.4s of No. 3 and 4 squadrons often operate from standby deployments, hidden in the woods around the base. They are assisted by the Puma helicopters of No. 230 Squadron, also based at Gütersloh. The Pumas are scheduled to be replaced by the new heavy-lift Chinooks of No. 18 Squadron in the near future.

Lured by lucrative coproduction deals and perhaps doubtful of design leadership in any European collaborative fighter program, four smaller NATO nations—Belgium, Norway, Denmark, and the Netherlands—bought into the General Dynamics F-16 program in the "Deal of the Century."

The first nation other than the United States to fly the Fighting Falcon was Belgium, whose No. 349 Escadrille was the first operational European F-16 squadron. They were joined later by No. 350e, also with No. 1 Wing, based at Beauvechain, near Waterloo. The next wing to convert to the F-16 will be No. 10 at Kleine Brugel, near the Dutch border. When the wing's No. 21 and 31 *escadrilles* (or *smaldelen,* as the Flemish say in bilingual Belgium) trade their F-104Gs for F-16s they will maintain Belgium's nuclear commitment to NATO.

The remainder of the combat aircraft of the Force Aerienne Belge, or Belgische Luchtmacht, are dedicated to the ground attack mission. No. 3 Wing, at Bierset, flies Mirage VBs, divided between its two squadrons, No. 1e and 8e. A companion wing, No. 2 at Florennes in the south, also operates the Mirage VBs, with No. 2e tasked for ground attack and No. 42e flying reconnaissance missions with its Mirage VBRs.

The Royal Danish Air Force, or *Kongelige Danske Flyvevaben* (KDF), has also received F-16s, to replace the old F-100s of *eskadrilles* 727 and 730 at Skrydstrup, near the German border. Like the Canadians, the Danish refuse to have anything to do with nuclear weapons. Their F-16s will be used for air-to-air and antishipping missions.

The rest of the KDF is badly in need of modernization. The "Huns" were old enough, but the balance of the Danish combat air force consists of aging Saab Drakens and F-104s. The Drakens are based at Karup, in central Denmark, with Eskadrille 725 flying attack F-35s while Eskadrille 729 uses its RF-35s in the recce role. Up north at Aalborg, Eskadrilles 723 and 726 operate their F-104s for interception, training, and ECM duties.

Farther south, the *Koninklijke Luchtmacht* (KLu), the Royal Netherlands Air Force, is also converting to the new Fighting Falcon. The KLu's first F-16s were delivered to No. 322 Squadron at Leeuwarden, near the North Sea coast. A companion unit, No. 323 Squadron, began receiving their Fighting Falcons shortly thereafter.

Other Dutch units due to convert from the F-104 to the F-16 are No. 306, No. 311, and No. 312 squadrons, based at Volkel, near Eindhoven. With the changeover, No. 311 and No. 312 squadrons will forfeit their nuclear strike commitment to NATO, the F-16s being considered more valuable in the interception role. The Netherlands will retain its nuclear capability in the form of Lance battlefield missiles, having unsuccessfully tried to divest itself of any nuclear role. The other Volkel squadron, No. 306, will retain its reconnaissance mission, moving south to De Peel in wartime.

Since the KLu base at Eindhoven is scheduled to close, its resident squadron, the NF-5-equipped No. 314, is being relocated to Gilze-Rijen, northwest of Tilburg. There it will join No. 316 Squadron, similarly equipped and also dedicated to the attack mission. Two other NF-5 units are based at Twenthe on the eastern border, just across the Reichswald from Hopsten/Laarbruch: No. 315 Squadron is another attack unit, and No. 313 is the NF-5 operational conversion training squadron.

The Luftwaffe maintains a presence in the NATO air forces second only to USAFE. Luftwaffe bases are concentrated in the north and south of Germany, allocated to 2 ATAF and 4 ATAF, respectively. More than that of any other nation, the German air force subordinates its peacetime operations to NATO command.

Each Luftwaffe air wing, or *geschwader,* consists of two squadrons, called *staffeln.* Each staffel has about twenty-four aircraft and pilots and is designated by the wing number and 1 or 2—No. 34 geschwader, for example, would have two squadrons, No. 341 and 342 staffeln. The flying group commander, the nearest Luftwaffe equivalent to a USAFE wing commander, is an *oberst,* a full colonel. His squadron counterpart, the *staffelkapitaen,* is usually a junior major.

The wings are also designated by mission. Most F-104 wings are *jagdbombergeschwader* (JBG), or fighter-bomber wings. The *jabos* (YAH-boes), as the pilots are called, are nonnuclear attack specialists, trained for low-altitude visual delivery of CBUs (cluster bomb units) or high-drag bombs, either straight and level or in a shallow dive. The jabos use "template" attacks, standardized tactics that split the attackers off an initial point, assigning them a particular curving course to the target.

There are four F-104 jabo wings. JBG 31 Boelcke is at Norvenich, near Köln (the name "Boelcke" is part of the geschwader's official designation, one of the four Luftwaffe wings named in honor of German air heroes, three from World War I and one, Mölders, from World War II). The other jabo wings are in 4 ATAF: JBG 32 at

Panavia Tornado Air Defense Variant. The basic version of the Tornado is entering service with the British, Italian, and German forces. Photo: British Aerospace

Lechfeld, west of Munich; JBG 33 at Büchel, just north of Hahn; and JBG 34 at Memmingen, west of Lechfeld.

The Luftwaffe, like many NATO air forces, has concentrated on the attack mission at the expense of air superiority. The situation was somewhat rectified with the acquisition of four wings of F-4Fs, a special version of the Phantom built for the Luftwaffe. Called "Elefants" by their aircrews, the F-4Fs are lighter than F-4Es, but lack the fire control radar for the Sparrow missiles and are armed with the Vulcan cannon and AIM-9Ls. The two *jagdgeschwader* —fighter wings, whose pilots are called *jaegers* (YAY-gurs), or hunters— are JG 71 Richthofen, at Wittmundenhafen in the northwest, and JG 74 Mölders, at Neuberg, near Ingolstadt. There are two other F-4F wings, but they are jabos; JBG 35 is at Pferdsfeld, between Ramstein and Hahn; JBG 36 is at Hopsten, next to RAF Laarbruch.

The rest of the Luftwaffe Phantom units fly the RF-4F and are *Aufklärungsgeschwader,* reconnaissance wings. AG 51 Immelmann is at Bremgarten, near Basel and the French-German-Swiss border; AG 52 is at Leck, near the Danish border.

The designation *"leichtenkampfgeschwader"* (LKG), or light attack wing, has disappeared with the retirement of G.91s in favor of the new Alpha Jet's introduction into Luftwaffe service. The two remaining "Gina" wings have converted to the

Alpha Jet and are now jabos: JBG 41s at Husum, south of Leck, and JBG 43s at Oldenburg, near the north German city of the same name. JBG 49, at Fürstenfeldbruck is also currently flying Alpha Jets—it's the operational conversion unit (OCU) for the new type.

The Luftwaffe OCU for the Tornado will be Waffenschule 10 at Jever, also home of the AAFCE Tactical Leadership Program. The German version of the Tornado is flying at the Tri-National Tornado Training Establishment at RAF Cottesmore, and eventually it will come into the hands of JBG 34 at Memmingen. When the jabos of 31, 33, and 32 JBGs make the transition to the new type, it will signal the end of the long and controversial career of the Starfighter in German service.

The F–104G's woes have been well documented: Over two hundred Luftwaffe and Marineflieger Starfighters have been lost since its introduction in 1961. Some experts suggest the German F–104 loss rate is not unusual, especially when compared with other fighters of its generation. The Luftwaffe, in fact, had better luck than most other Starfighter operators—Canada had a loss rate almost twice as large, proportionately, while Italy and the United States had comparable losses (the accident rate was one of the reasons the F–104 never caught on with the USAF).

But it was the German Starfighter that caught the world's attention. For one thing, it was the first "Deal of the Century," the opening up of a potentially huge arms market in rebuilt Germany, with the added incentive that whichever plane the Luftwaffe chose the smaller NATO nations would surely adopt as well. The sale was fraught with allegations of bribes and bad feeling, but the truth is there was not much else to choose from at the time (although the Marineflieger had wanted the Buccaneer).

The thing that really got the "Starfighter Scandals" going was the fact that the F–104 loss rate did not decline, but actually *increased* as time

went by. Thirty Starfighters were lost in 1965, almost one every ten days. Called "the missile with a man in it," the F–104 soon gained more grim nicknames—"Flying Coffin" and "Widow Maker." The "Starfighter Widows" were actually among the plane's most vocal critics.

The F–104G (for Germany) was one of the hottest airplanes of its day, certainly the most complicated aircraft ever flown by the new Luftwaffe. It was so much advanced over the model that had such a brief and unhappy career in American service that it was designated the "Super Starfighter," although the superlative soon faded from use.

But the single-engined superfighter was little suited to the German style of low-level operation. Gen. Johannes Steinhoff, then Inspector of the Luftwaffe, wrote that the Starfighter was "forever jealous of the pilot's full attention. It rewarded discipline with deeds of airmanship; it could punish the dilatory or those who gave themselves to distractions. It was marvelous in capable hands and merciless to the careless."

Canada, Japan, the Netherlands, Italy, Belgium, Denmark, and Norway bought Starfighters as well, and three of those countries—Canada, the Netherlands, and Norway—also bought F–5As, another American-designed export fighter.

The sale of American aircraft in Europe has always been controversial, and everybody has something to say about it. The larger European nations complain that the sales are hurting the chances of ever developing a viable European aircraft industry, and they accuse the Americans of selling less capable aircraft than they would use in their own USAF. The smaller NATO nations say there's no way they could develop the aircraft themselves and are wary of being "junior partners" in collaborative programs with the larger European countries. At least with the Americans they can arrange to build competitive aircraft under license and keep their domestic aircraft industry going. The Americans say that the smaller nations are

free to choose whichever planes they want, and see the sales as a way to get back a fraction of the costs of their defense commitment to NATO.

The truth is, it's just getting too damned expensive to develop modern combat aircraft. As national budgets are shrunk by inflation and development costs increase geometrically, money *is* an object, for the first time in the history of air warfare. NATO nations, hit hard by the cost of recent aircraft projects—all reasonably well managed—are extremely nervous about the future.

They have a right to be. The two biggest drains on any national budget these days are energy and defense. Imagine how hard life would be for a prime minister who had to choose between oil and airplanes. Many NATO leaders are faced with that choice today.

Let's return to the NATO numbers game and see if we can make sense of it now:

Royal Navy Sea Harrier VTOL jets turned in astonishing performances in the Falklands conflict. GR. 3 Harriers are land-based at RAF Gutersloh, Germany. Photo: British Aerospace

In central Europe, NATO aircraft are outnumbered by Warsaw Pact aircraft by about 1.5, or 2 to 1. Although NATO aircraft are presently qualitatively superior to Warsaw Pact aircraft, the lack of any clear-cut plans for a new generation of NATO aircraft leaves the question of future superiority very much in doubt. National rivalries and conflicting needs make cohesive NATO aircraft development difficult, although a well-organized command structure and the pride and professionalism of the various national air forces make command integration workable. But none of this exists in a vacuum. Let's take a look at what the other side is up to.

Chapter 8
The Soviet Union and the Warsaw Pact: Bogeys and Bandits

According to one expert on Soviet aviation, the greatest thing about the Russian air forces, from a writer's point of view, is that you can say anything you want about them and it's bound to be true.

Quite right! The air forces of the Soviet Union are full of contradictions and unanswered questions: They spend billions on cheap airplanes. Their pilots are a highly trained elite but lack individual initiative. The Russian air forces are the most formidable collection of men and machines in the world—on paper—but the Soviet Union hasn't fought a real war since 1945.

One source of misconception is a problem of perception: mirror-imaging. We know what our aircraft are built to do, what our tactics and missions are, and we expect the Soviets to be the same. We judge them on our terms, so it's no wonder they sometimes come up short. Or as one Bitburg fighter pilot puts it:

The American public has an unwarranted sense of security in that they think the Russians build airplanes that don't do this and they don't do that because we build airplanes that can do all kinds of things.

I think when the Russians decide to build an airplane they say, "What do we want it to do?" and then they build an airplane that can do that one thing really well, but it doesn't do anything else very well at all.

That was the way it used to be, anyway. While the USAF built multirole fighter-bombers like the F–4, capable of handling just about any type of mission, the Soviets built cheaper, less-sophisticated point-defense interceptors like the MiG–17, MiG–19, and MiG–21. They were limited in multimission capability, but as American pilots who tangled with them over North Vietnam tell it, the MiGs did their one job—air defense—very well.

But there's been a significant change in the last generation of combat aircraft. The American and Soviet philosophies have switched; the USAF now goes in for more specialized designs—the air-superiority F–15 and the close air support A–10, for example—while the Russians have started to build multirole fighter-bombers like their Flogger series.

This is indicative of a new and disturbing trend in the Soviet air forces. Traditionally, the Russians have concentrated on short-range fighters and surface-to-air missiles; the main goal was to keep opposing air power off the backs of their ground forces. But the Soviets are now going from *defense* to *offense*, and this is reflected in their latest generation of aircraft.

USAFE pilots don't lose a great deal of sleep worrying about the MiG–23 Flogger and its newer stablemate, the Su–24 Fencer strike aircraft. They have a healthy respect for them, but it is generally conceded that the Fencer and the Flogger repre-

MiG-25 Foxbat A in Libyan markings. Hard points carry AA-6 Acrid air-to-air missiles. Debut of the Foxbat in the late sixties sparked USAF development of the F-15. *Photo: U.S. Navy*

sent technology on a level with the aging F-4 Phantom. But they *are* concerned with two developments: the sheer number of Warsaw Pact aircraft and the new Soviet designs due to enter service soon.

First the numbers:

"They've got lots of them," says a senior officer at Bitburg.

They're producing the Flogger at the rate of over six hundred a year—that could re-equip all of the wings in Germany in one year.

Now, would I like to have twice as many F-15s? Hell yes I would, because we're greatly outnumbered by the other side. We have to be able to kill in a ratio of four or five to one to be able to even the odds. *It's realistic. We could do that, but I don't like those kinds of odds, because—other than the Israelis—it's been shown when you're outnumbered in the air-to-air arena over a long period of time you have a tough time winning.*

USAFE pilots are also apprehensive about the new types of aircraft under development in the

Soviet Union. The USAF has just undergone a major re-equipment program in the last decade with the F-15, F-16, and A-10 and has no concrete production plans for any new combat aircraft. On the other hand, the Soviet Union is reportedly developing four new fighters, a new close air support aircraft, and three new bombers.

"I don't think we're going to build too many more new airplanes, so if they can outdo what we've got right now . . ." muses an F-15 jock at Bitburg.

They continually improve. They're like the Japanese were—remember a long time ago, when everybody said if it's made in Japan it's probably not very good? Now if it's made in Japan it costs twice as much and it's just great.

Their state-of-the-art aircraft right now are much different than they were. There's not a lot we can talk about, but I don't think the American public is aware of their technological development, how far along they really are, that they can do the things I can't tell you they can do.

Spy stuff. One supposes, or rather hopes, that the Air Force knows more about the new Russian aircraft than they're saying. To be sure, it's always difficult to divulge juicy details about the enemy without somehow revealing where the information came from. Besides, the intelligence community has been burned before on the tricky business of evaluating new Soviet aircraft.

Take, for example, the MiG-25, at first thought to be so fierce an air-to-air fighter that the F-15 project took on the atmosphere of a crash program as the United States struggled to "catch up" to the Mach 3 Foxbat. As more became known about the Mig-25, the super fighter turned into a flying dog, with the aerodynamics and turning ability of a falling refrigerator. It was only with the defection of Lt. Viktor Belenko and a close examination of his MiG-25P that the West began to evaluate the Foxbat in its true role—a rather crude but cleverly designed high-altitude interceptor somewhere between the F-15 and the SR-71,

but not quite like either one of them. Another problem of perception.

The MiG-25 was designed as a counter to the American B-70 Valkyrie, a high altitude, Mach 3 strategic bomber. But the B-70 project was canceled after the Foxbat was well into development. The United States had no need for an interceptor like the MiG-25 and was therefore puzzled by it. Mirror-imaging, again.

So the Air Force keeps quiet about the new Russian aircraft. What details have been published about them could have been garnered from reconnaissance satellites—nothing secret about that. Let's take a look.

Already reportedly deployed in two operational regiments is the latest version of the MiG-25, dubbed the "Foxhound." Observed at the Soviet testing range at Vladimirovka, the Foxhound carried eight AA-9 missiles and a newer, more powerful radar. It has reportedly demonstrated a formidable look-down shoot-down capability, although some Western analysts are doubtful about the aircraft's ability to pick cruise missile-size targets out of clutter. But they have been wrong before.

Other aircraft have reportedly been spotted at the Soviet flight test center at Ramenskoye and have accordingly been given the prefix "RAM."

RAM-J is a dedicated close air support aircraft often compared to the American A-10, although it is somewhat smaller and it is not known whether or not it is armored. It does have a 30-mm Gatling cannon in the nose, a fact that has disturbed American analysts. (At least one A-10 pilot intimates that the United States has passed up the chance to sell the Warthog overseas because of a reluctance to export the gun technology.)

As with most aircraft designs, the Russians are again accused of copying the Americans, but it must be remembered the Soviet Union pioneered the type back in World War II with the Shturmovik.

There was another attempt at a Soviet close air support aircraft in the fifties, with the Ilyushin Il-40 Brawny, but the RAM-J is the first modern successor to the Shturmovik. The RAM-J is now known to be a product of the Sukhoi bureau, and is more often referred to as the "Su-25." The first Su-25 squadron is already operational and has reportedly seen action in Afghanistan.

The RAM-K is reportedly a Sukhoi design, a twin-engined, swing-wing air-superiority fighter. Called a "Super MiG-23," the RAM-K might be the long-awaited advanced Soviet fighter referred to as "Fearless" in the software of USAF flight simulators.

In planform the RAM-K bears a suspicious resemblance to the American Tomcat, causing defense analysts to believe the Soviets have gotten hold of at least the F-14 engineering drawings, if not the real thing—from Iran.

The third fighter, the RAM-L, is an F-18 look-alike, generally conceded to be a Mikoyan product. With its copycat design and bubble canopy, the RAM-L is the most "American"-looking of all the new prototypes. Although it is probably an air-superiority interceptor destined to replace the aging Su-15, the RAM-L has been suggested in the Japanese aviation press as a marine fighter for a new class of Soviet conventional-deck aircraft carrier, but that is the most speculative of all this speculation. A modified MiG-27 and an advanced version of the Soviet Naval VTOL (vertical takeoff and landing) Forger have also been promoted as candidates for this "new carrier," with little proof that the ship, let alone the planes, are under consideration by the Soviets.

The Russians are also supposedly developing three new bombers: a four-engined cruise missile carrier, a slightly redesigned "Super Backfire" and an all-out intercontinental bomber capable of reaching targets in the United States supersonically at low level. But the Soviets have been developing, and scrapping, bomber designs for the better part of a decade—including a reported Sukhoi delta-winged design and a military version of the TU-144 supersonic transport—trying, apparently without success, to come up with something that would be a significant improvement in range and capability over their highly successful Backfire medium bomber.

In fact, it is difficult to say how many of the proto-types will actually enter production. The Russians have a history of refining experimental aircraft to a fine edge, only to discard them at the last stages of development. At the famous Domodedovo Air Show of 1967 the Soviets introduced no less than twelve new types or variants of aircraft unknown to the West, including the MiG-23, MiG-25, Su-17, and Su-15. Right now, it looks as if the RAM-K, now called the Su-27, and the RAM-L, referred to as the MiG-29, are headed for produc-tion, but there is no accurate published projection as to where or when they will enter operational service. What is certain—and is making USAFE pilots a bit anxious—is that the Soviets are devel-oping many new types of aircraft and the United States isn't.

The Soviet Union is also reported to be working up two military versions of its commercial Il-76 Candid transport: a tanker and an airborne com-mand and control aircraft. The latter, designated the SUAWACS, for Soviet Union Airborne Early Warning and Control System, is the long-awaited successor to the Tu-126 Moss, called "The Spider" by Pakistani intelligence during the Indo-Pakistani War.

In typical fashion, Western analysts have bad-mouthed the Moss as ineffective and talked up the SUAWACS as a convincing answer to the E-3A Sentry. In reality, the Moss and the SUAWACS are probably progressively more advanced airborne early warning planes—radar pickets designed to patrol the Soviet Union's interminable borders. The SUAWACS is more likely to be, at best, barely on a level with the Navy's E-2C Hawkeye.

Of more immediate concern to USAFE pilots is the introduction of much advanced air-to-air missiles in the Soviet inventory. For the first time, the Russians now have an all-aspect capability that must be respected, a capability that will improve with the new AA–XP–1 and AA–XP–2 missiles now under development. It is hard to overestimate the impact this little-publicized but vital development has in the central European air combat arena. USAFE pilots can no longer feel safe just by checking their six—danger can now come from any point on the compass, well beyond visual range. And even though the Soviet all-aspect missiles, even the ones under development, are probably not as advanced as American missiles, it's going to be much tougher for Western pilots from now on.

The Russians are also developing a wide range of air-to-surface munitions for their new offensive role. The Soviet Union was impressed by the performance of American precision-guided munitions (PGM)—"smart bombs"—in the later stages of the Vietnam War and have developed laser and electro-optical PGM and air-to-surface missiles for use on their recently introduced attack aircraft. But they're still interested in "dumb bombs" and have developed cluster munitions, fuel-air explosives, larger unguided rockets, and a new airfield attack weapon called the "Dibber." The latter may be similar to the British JP–233, a particularly nasty weapon that reportedly craters up runways with a powerful warhead and then uses delayed action submunitions to injure any workers attempting repairs. Royal Naval Sea Harriers reportedly used JP–233s in their attacks on Argentine airfields in the Falkland Islands.

The Soviet Union maintains a mighty army, an expanding navy, and in terms of numbers, the world's most powerful air force. The Voyenno-Vozdushnyye Sily (V-VS), the battlefield air arm of the Soviet Union, consists of over a million men and between ten and fifteen thousand aircraft.

The Soviet air forces are controlled by the General Staff and are divided into three parts: air defense, naval aviation, and the V-VS, which operates the bomber, transport, and tactical air commands.

The Voyska Protivovozdushanoy Oborony Strany (P-VO Strany), or air defense of the homeland, has almost as many personnel as the entire USAF. Istrebitel'naya Aviatsia, the fighter command of the P-VO Strany, operates just about every interceptor in the Soviet inventory but still uses the Su–15 as its primary front-line fighter. The ground component of the P-VO Strany has three subsections: the "Zenith" missile, antiaircraft artillery troops, and the radar operators.

The P-VO Strany is somewhat comparable to the old USAF Air Defense Command, although much larger. Indeed, in recent organizational changes, the P-VO Strany has gotten *larger,* absorbing air defense units formerly under Red Army command.

The Aviatsia Voenno-Morskogo Flota (AV-MF) is the Soviet naval aviation command, one of the fastest-growing segments of Soviet air power. The AV-MF is perhaps the prime user of the Backfire, as well as the highly important Bear-D electronic warfare and command control platform. There is also a growing interest in carrier aviation—the Soviet Union has three new VTOL carriers equipped with antisubmarine helicopters and the Yak–36, although a replacement for the comparatively harmless Forger is undoubtedly in the works.

The V-VS has its own SAC and MAC type organizations, the Dal'naya Aviatsia (DA) and the Voenno-Transportnaya Aviatsia (V-TA), respectively. DA, or Long Range Aviation, took on a new life with the introduction of the Backfire and promises to become even more important as the Soviet Union concentrates on long-range bombers to compensate for its deficiency in cruise-missile technology. V-TA is closely allied with the Soviet flag carrier, Aeroflot (in fact, in the old days, Aeroflot used to fly airliners with tailguns, a decidedly Russian innovation).

But by far the most important V-VS command, from a central European standpoint, is the Frontovaya Aviatsia (FA). Frontal Aviation is often compared to TAC, the Tactical Air Command of the USAF, and there are similarities—FA is the conventional battlefield air arm of the V-VS, home of aces and star of the budget, where new aircraft types are first introduced. But FA is much more closely allied with the ground operations than is TAC.

FA is split into tactical air armies, each with an average of three *divisiya,* or divisions, although the number can vary widely from as many as nine divisions to just one. The division is broken down into three regiments, or *polki.* A *polk* is the nearest Soviet equivalent to an American wing, but has less aircraft; fighter regiments have an average of forty aircraft, ground-attack regiments slightly fewer. Soviet squadrons are smaller as well, with each of the three *eskadrilii* numbering about twelve aircraft. There are three flights *(zveno)* in each squadron.

In addition to the tactical air armies of the Soviet military districts, the FA also provides air support for the Soviet Union's four "Groups of Forces" in selected Warsaw Pact countries: Poland (headquartered at Legnice), Czechoslovakia (Milovice), and Hungary (Tokal, near Budapest). But the largest of these is the Group of Soviet Forces in Germany; its 16th Tactical Air Army is the most powerful FA subunit and the nearest Soviet equivalent to the United States Air Forces in Europe.

From its headquarters at Zossen-Wunsdorf, the 16th operates almost eight hundred fighters and fighter-bombers, mostly Su-17 Fitters, MiG-21 Fishbeds, MiG-23 Floggers, and MiG-27 Flogger Ds, the dedicated ground attack variant called "Ducknose" by its pilots because of its redesigned forward fuselage. The MiG-21, uprated into abstraction, remains in front-line Soviet service, more a tribute to the air-to-air deficiencies

and poor rate of production of the MiG-23, its scheduled successor, than to its own capabilities.

When it was first introduced, the Fishbed was a highly effective dogfighter. It is still quite capable, although no match for modern American fighters in terms of range, electronics, and sustained maneuverability (the MiG-21's novel tailed-delta configuration makes for a good initial turn capability, but it loses energy much faster than the clipped-delta F-15s and F-16s). The Flogger has turned out to be much less agile than expected—its variable-geometry wings are not swung in combat like the F-14s but are instead used only for takeoffs and landings, and in loiter, to conserve fuel. The MiG-21s *are* being phased out in favor of the MiG-23 but at a much slower rate than first expected, not only because the Flogger is not as fierce a fighter as first feared, but also due to a failure of the much-vaunted Soviet production capacity to produce the MiG-23 in numbers sufficient to replace the herds of Fishbeds in Soviet service. The still formidable MiG-21 continues to form the backbone of most Warsaw Pact fighter units.

There are no Su-24 Fencers stationed in Germany, but in wartime some Su-24 regiments would probably deploy from their bases in eastern Europe—in fact, a Fencer unit operated from Templin in East Germany on a recent exercise.

The 16th Tactical Air Army is divided into two air corps. The Northern Air Corps is headquartered at Wittstock, with regiments from its fighter division based at Wittstock, Puttnitz, and Gross-Dolln. The corps' fighter-bomber division has Su-17 and MiG-27 regiments at Rechlin-Larz, Neuruppen, and Parchim.

The Southern Air Corps, headquartered at Wittenberg, is even more powerful, with two fighter divisions and a fighter-bomber division. The six fighter bases in the Southern Air Corps are at Jüterbog, Zerbst, and Köthen, and Merseburg, Altenburg, and Alt-Lunnewitz. The regiments of the fighter-bomber division are based at Brusin, Finow, and Werneuchen.

In addition to the Floggers and Fitters, the 16th has a number of specialized reconnaissance and ECM aircraft, including the recce version of the Foxbat and an electronic warfare variant of the ancient Yak–28 Brewer. The unit also operates attack helicopters, including the newer Hind helicopter gunships, from Parchim and Stendal air bases.

Add to this the air armies supporting the other three groups of Soviet forces in Europe, the air armies of the military districts of eastern Russia, and the air forces of the Warsaw Pact, and it's easy to see why USAFE commanders are nervous about numbers.

On the other hand, no other Soviet air army is nearly as powerful as the 16th, sometimes referred to as the *Elite* Frontal Aviation Army. And the air forces of the Warsaw Pact nations are much more poorly equipped, with few of the new fighter-bombers being introduced in front-line Soviet service. The new aircraft *have* been sold, albeit in less capable variants, to foreign nations considered vital to Soviet interests. Paradoxically, Czech and East German pilots often serve as instructors (and, reportedly, sometimes more) in countries where the Soviet Union exercises "MiG Diplomacy."

Soviet and Warsaw Pact air bases, like their NATO counterparts, have undergone a tone-down program to make them less visible from the air. The Warsaw Pact bases are also constructing hardened aircraft shelters but in this they lag behind the West, and a tempting percentage of their aircraft are parked in revetments or even out in the open. Although their aircraft are, on the whole, capable of operating from strips much cruder than those NATO aircraft are accustomed to, their older models are tied to ground equipment and many still need auxiliary generators to start engines.

Not much is known about the general layout of Soviet fighter bases, although it is doubtful they house the movie theaters and pizza bars found on many USAFE bases. About the closest they come to comfort is the squadron's Lenin Room, where the pilot-heroes hang out before hopping into the cool green cockpits of their Floggers and going off to mock battle with the Flying Gangsters and other Dark Forces of the West.

The Soviet pilot is a mystery to most Americans. Even USAFE jocks have a tough time sorting him out. On one hand, they know he is a member of the Communist elite, well trained and educated, the cream of a society that appears to hold martial and scientific values above all others. On the other hand, they know Soviet pilots average less flight time than most American pilots; and even though their aircraft are less complex, their training missions are far less demanding.

Although Western pilots do exercise more initiative in the air-to-air arena, there is no reason to believe every Soviet fighter jock is a automaton (or, as they say in the Air Force, a "Cylon Clone at the MiG's controls," an allusion to the rather dimwitted, red-eyed, chrome-plated robots of television's *Battlestar Galactica* series). It's true that, traditionally, Soviet doctrine requires most missions be flown under positive ground control, with the added provision that if contact with the ground controllers is lost the mission is to be aborted.

But USAFE pilots also spend a lot of time on the radio with controllers—more time than they would like, but that's another story. At any rate, the latest Soviet doctrine does allow for more initiative by pilots, especially in close air combat. Still, the USAF spends much more time and money educating fighter pilots than the Russians do, and the new highly realistic training regimen introduced to American pilots after the Vietnam War has no equal in the East.

We know about this latest Soviet tactical development because of a series of articles that appeared in the Soviet magazine *Aviation and Cosmonautics* during the summer of 1978. Since

Aviatsiya i Kosmonaytika is a government publication, as are all Soviet magazines, it must be carefully analyzed before realistic conclusions can be drawn.

The series, written by staff writer Col. V. Dubrov, is titled "How Was Air Combat Changed?" and examines air warfare during the latest regional conflicts, especially the Vietnam War and those in the Middle East. The articles are particularly fascinating in that they contain veiled admiration of Western air theory and even some implied criticism of Soviet doctrine, although this is usually attributed to "foreign experts."

The articles divide air combat into five segments: search, closing, attack, maneuver, and disengagement. In the search phase, Colonel Dubrov states that the importance of visual acquisition was re-emphasized in Vietnam—new tail-warning and airborne radars, as well as IFF systems, proved unreliable and often failed at the critical moment. (Curiously, he does not mention the Rules of Engagement USAF pilots had to follow that usually required visual identification of targets before firing long-range radar missiles.) He does say, not surprisingly, that flying under positive ground control increases a pilot's chances of success.

Colonel Dubrov defines closing as the conversion from sighting to the attack position, which involves concealment and swiftness. Since World War II—like all Russians, he calls it the Great Patriotic War—swiftness has become more important than concealment, as radar makes it harder to sneak up on an opponent. A high thrust-to-weight ratio is the most important ingredient in swiftness of closing, as it indicates a rapid rate of acceleration. Most of the new Soviet fighters are alleged to have a thrust-to-weight ratio of greater than one-to-one.

In the attack segment, Colonel Dubrov cites surprise and the success of the first pass as the key elements in air-to-air combat. He estimates that 75 percent of all kills in World War II were achieved on the first pass, 15 percent on the second, and only 10 percent on the third, and says "foreign experts" found the figures remained constant in Vietnam and the Middle East.

Colonel Dubrov goes on to say that although surprise has been harder to achieve in modern air combat, the consequences of *being* surprised are more severe. With the new generation of all-aspect missiles employed by both sides, attack may now be initiated on a turning approach, instead of the uniformly straight-ahead attacks of the Vietnam era.

The increased agility of modern fighters and missiles makes a fourth segment, maneuver, inevitable. This is the "dogfight" so dear to the heart of American pilots. Colonel Dubrov dismisses it as almost counterproductive: "We should note," he writes, "that a swift series of maneuvers and point-blank fire at a vigorously evading adversary is a picture characteristic of only one fourth of successful engagements."

Although he prefers the one-pass-and-out Soviet style of air combat, Colonel Dubrov recognizes there are times—after a failed first pass, for example, or when a target pops up too close to use missiles—when the pilot must stay and fight or be shot down trying to escape.

Accordingly, Colonel Dubrov seems to agree with the "experts" he cites as labeling these dogfights "defensive combat." The close-in engagement, he says, is governed by the defender when the element of surprise is blown. The attacker cannot use his long-range missiles and must be content to tail the defender and mirror his maneuvers.

The colonel goes on to say some bad things about USAF air-to-air training in the Vietnam War and some good things about the newer American aircraft (especially the F–16), before coming to some conclusions about dogfights:

Colonel Dubrov says recent air-to-air combat is not all that different from World War II dogfights, that good flying ability, high G tolerance, situational awareness, and gunnery skills are the most important elements of pilot success, and that, given equal aircraft and abilities, the dogfight will be won by the "illogical" (unpredictable) maneuver. That's as clear an assessment of air-to-air combat as has ever been written.

The disengagement phase has often been a problem, as many aircraft have been shot down trying to leave a fight. Colonel Dubrov describes the separation maneuvers used by the USAF in Vietnam but contributes little to the discussion himself, except the rather obvious statement that "the disengagement phase should only be considered complete after the aircraft have landed."

But Colonel Dubrov has something to say to all of us, something every instant analyst and mirror-image specialist should keep in mind when discussing Soviet air power.

"As is noted abroad," says the colonel, "the tendency to underestimate the adversary's capabilities in order to push through one's own ideas is rather widespread and has shown its faultiness in local wars."

Soviet Aircraft Designations

Contrary to misconceptions fostered in the popular press, not all Soviet warplanes are called "MiGs." Although the design collective of Artem I. Mikoyan and Mikhail I. Gurevich is the most successful and well-known Russian *Opytno-Konstruktorskoye Byuro* ("Experimental Construction Bureau"—OKB), the Soviet air forces are made up of the products of many other OKB. But, since the bureaus tend to specialize, and since the fighters from the Mikoyan-Gurevich collective have most often met Western fighters in combat, MiGs tend to grab most of the attention.

Running a close second in importance to the Soviet air forces is the design collective of Pavel A. Sukhoi. Like most Russian OKB, the Sukhoi bureau can trace its origins back to before World War II. Although it has created a series of interceptors for the PVO-Strany, the Sukhoi collective's main contribution to the tactical air arms has been in the form of ground-attack aircraft—the long-running Fitter series and the new and terrible Su-24 Fencer.

The other bureaus tend to build larger or more specialized aircraft. The design collective of Andrei N. Tupolev builds large, multi-engined bombers, including the Tu-26 Backfire. The bureaus of Sergei N. Ilyushin and Oleg K. Antonev build mainly transports and cargo aircraft, such as the new An-72 Coaler and the impressive Il-76 Candid. The design collective of Alexander S. Yakovlev seems now to specialize in vertical take-off and landing aircraft, such as the carrier-borne Yak-36 Forger.

The bureaus have changed quite a bit since their formation. The original OKB were small teams of scientists huddled about the drawing boards. They were often disbanded when their chief designer died or was forced out in disgrace. (Pavel Sukhoi was especially unlucky. Sukhoi, whose name literally means the "Dry One," suffered through a series of failures that were not his fault and lost his bureau. It was re-established in 1953, after Stalin died and everybody developed amnesia on a wide scale.)

Nowadays, the bureaus are huge operations, much more permanent and complex, and unlikely to be disbanded on a whim. Indeed, although most of the original chief designers are dead—Sukhoi died in 1975, Ilyushin in 1977 and Mikoyan in 1970, Gurevich having long since faded from the scene—their bureaus get bigger and bigger. Another fascinating note: In a land where every man's a comrade and there are supposed to be no favorites, two bureaus are headed by the sons of their founders and another former chief engineer's son is a test pilot.

Libyan MiG-23 Flogger E (Russia's export version) with Atoll heat-seeking missiles. *Photo: U.S. Navy*

Soviet planes are known by an OKB acronym and a two-digit number: odd numbers for tactical fighters and fighter bombers, even numbers for larger multi-engine bombers and transports. Unlike Western nations, which use sequential letters of the alphabet to denote substantial improvements in a basic airframe, the Soviet system is to use letters that stand for the specific improvement. Thus, a MiG-21F would be a re-engined fighter from the Mikoyan-Gurevich OKB's "21" series, the *F* standing for *forsirovanny,* or "boosted engine."

Soviet service designations are not published and accurate model numbers are often unknown to the West until they are exported or the Russians volunteer the information in treaty negotiations. To help clear up the confusion, NATO uses designations created by the Air Standards Coordinating Committee, a consortium of English-speaking countries. The committee's system is loosely based upon the method used by the United States to identify Japanese planes during World War II. As soon as a Soviet aircraft enters service it is given a reporting name that begins with the letter of its type—"F" for fighters, "B" for bombers, and so on. Reporting names for jet aircraft have two syllables, prop planes one. The names are supposed to be meaningless, or at the very least, derogatory, so we have jet fighters with names like "Flipper," "Flora," and—a personal favorite— "Faithless."

125

Chapter 9
The Future: Dreamland

Stealth! Silent, cool, and transparent. The very word conjures the black angel of death, shrouded in invisibility from the microwave's formerly omnipotent glare. Panic in eastern Europe: They can no longer trust their eyes, let alone their up-to-now dreaded Gyrotron Tube.

Like the aircraft it has developed, the Stealth program keeps a low profile and is hard to define. The buzz of controversy that surrounded the "announcement" of the project in the closing months of the Carter presidency produced more heat than light. The Stealth program was made public for reasons similar to President Johnson's disclosure in the 1960s of the then-secret SR-71 being developed at the Lockheed "Skunk Works" —certainly there were political considerations, but the biggest reason for going public was simply that the project was getting too big to hide in the budget (the United States spent about a billion dollars in Stealth research in 1981 alone).

Most of the information released at the time was obviously misleading, most of the "drawings" laughingly provisional. But a few details, picked up here and there from more technical sources, are fascinating.

To begin with, there is no such thing as "The Stealth Bomber," just as there is no one "Air-Superiority Fighter." Stealth is rather a collection of technologies, the principles of which are well known. The trick is putting them into an aircraft without sacrificing too much performance.

The USAF has apparently been experimenting with "low observables"—the insider's word for Stealth—since the early sixties. The idea is not to make an invisible aircraft, but rather to reduce its chances of being detected by sight, sound, infrared, or radar. Neither is the aircraft completely silent, without infrared signature or radar cross section. Early efforts showed it *was* possible, however, to develop an aircraft that had a much lower probability of detection by conventional means, but the cost—both financial and operational—wasn't worth putting the developmental aircraft into production.

The "low-visibility" camouflage schemes on the F-15 and F-16 are almost certainly fallout from early Stealth research. But it was discovered that to take best advantage of "low observables" it was necessary to build an aircraft with Stealth in mind from the ground up.

Lockheed reportedly built scaled-down demonstrator versions of its Stealth fighters under a project code-named Have Blue, funded by the Defense Advanced Research Projects Agency (DARPA). The test flights apparently took place during the late seventies and early eighties at a super-secret airfield known as "The Ranch." The strip is north of Las Vegas and Nellis Air Force Base, part of a large complex of restricted airfields and ranges called Dreamland (where, it is alleged, the USAF also flies Soviet-built MiGs).

Two of the Stealth demonstrators reportedly crashed, one of them killing the pilot. The accidents were blamed on a rush to get the aircraft into the air and on the hazards of test flying in general, rather than on any specific dangers re-

The latest thing? This canard-winged creature is Boeing's concept of a fighter aircraft applying the technology of commercial supersonic cruise aircraft. This configuration was designed for the European theater, with Mach-2 speed and a 500-mile combat radius. *Photo: Boeing*

lated to Stealth technology. Lockheed is supposedly now building twenty full-sized Stealth fighters. There is also work being done on two other Stealth aircraft—an advanced technology bomber and an air-launched cruise missile.

No photographs have ever been released of any Stealth aircraft, leading to all manner of jokes about "invisible airplanes" in the press. But given a crash course in low observables, we can put together a rough idea of what a "Stealth" aircraft would look like compared with the USAF's current front-line fighter, the F-15 Eagle.

The human eye can't see the turbine fan blades whirring in the intakes of the F-15 because of the shadows, but it's like waving a signal mirror to a radar. Neither can we see the F-15's radar an-

SR-71 Blackbird, used for ultra-high-speed, ultra-high-altitude reconnaissance missions. *Photo: Lockheed*

tenna hidden inside the nose cone, but since the radome is dielectric (it lets other radars see in just as easily as it sees out) the F-15's flat planar radar antenna looks like a hog's nose on our scope. The human eye sees right through the Eagle's round, clear canopy, but because it scatters and bounces the microwave energy in all directions it is a good radar reflector—the same goes for the Eagle's big, square air intakes. The missiles and pods slung underneath the F-15 are also hard to see head-on, but not for radar; underwing stores create a larger, though fuzzy, radar picture.

And since—all other factors being equal—an arithmetic increase in size tends to lead to an almost geometric increase in radar cross section, the Eagle is too big to be a "Stealth Fighter." But perhaps the biggest drawback of the F-15 in terms of radar signature is the way it's shaped. Right-angle intersections of metal produce a radar picture much larger than their actual size. So-called corner reflectors are used to take advan-

tage of this inherent quality of radar. They are flown on small drone aircraft to simulate a much larger plane and thus give radar operators realistic practice. The Eagle is a symphony of right angles and therefore flunks our "Stealth Test."

Okay, so what does a Stealth fighter look like? Let's go back to the Eagle and reconstruct it using low observables.

The turbine blades offer the radar metal and motion—its favorite sights—so the intakes must snake back to the engines in a more circumspect fashion. And we'll put the intake up on top of the aircraft to shield it from the ground radar. Effective fighter radar antennae are always going to be big and flat, but we can mask it behind frequency-sensitive radomes, metallic nose cones that are permeable only to the emissions from the aircraft's radar and block all others. We'll replace the bubble canopy with a canopy of flat panes, like those in helicopter gunships, to deflect microwave energy evenly, up and away from the radar receiver. We'll also get rid of the pylons and underwing stores—anything this aircraft carries will have to be stashed inside the airframe.

Our Stealth aircraft is smaller than the F-15, but then so is almost every other fighter in the world. We defeat the "corner reflector" by "rounding out" the airplane, that is, eliminating the sharp metal corners and joining the wings and tails with the fuselage as smoothly as possible. The best planform combining life and maneuverability would seem to be a delta, but we have to be careful about it, clipping off the corners and blending the wing in with leading edge extensions.

Based on Stealth technology and the little information from the popular press that can be trusted, this is what a Stealth aircraft probably looks like: about the size of an F-18, with twin inward-leaning tails, an intake mounted above the fuselage, a segmented F-106-type canopy, a metallic radome, no pylons or external stores, and an extended delta wing with rounded corners. The Stealth prototype is said to have a planform like that of the Space Shuttle, and a profile similar to the SR-71.

But what color is it? Remember, the original Stealth program also investigated ways of making the aircraft less visible, and to this end they experimented with such bizarre schemes as "mirror" camouflage—highly reflective paint that helped the aircraft blend in with its background. They also tested the possibility of shining lights on various parts of the aircraft to remove the shadows the eye uses for visual cues of an aircraft's attitude.

But low visibility is not nearly as important as a low radar cross section to the Stealth aircraft's mission, and it is reasonable to believe the aircraft are left unpainted. This is because any sort of paint might interfere with the radar-absorbent materials doubtlessly used in the aircraft's construction.

Radar-absorbent materials trap microwave emissions instead of allowing them to bounce back from the aircraft and into the radar receiver. Although such materials have been around a long time, they have always been too heavy, too expensive, or—as the Navy found out when it experimented with submarine periscopes coated with radar-absorbent materials—they tended to break up too quickly under stress. But new breakthroughs may make it possible to use radar-absorbent materials in the aircraft's construction rather than sticking them on as a coating, thus solving many wear and weight problems.

So the Stealth aircraft probably do not do it with mirrors or lights and are more likely to be the dull gray color of most modern combat aircraft. Or they might be the dark indigo blue—really black—of the SR-71, considering the altitudes and speeds at which they will be flying.

The Stealth mission profile is a giant step backward: high speed, high altitude penetration. Modern air defenses, which chased everyone down to low-level, are now chasing them back into the heavens. Flying above 50,000 feet takes the aircraft out of the range of most missiles and anti-aircraft artillery and to the pilots' great relief, every "Golden BB." If enemy radars can be rendered useless, high altitude attackers will be virtually immune from danger.

We all know this is not the way the world works. No aircraft, not even the Stealth aircraft, are completely invisible. Only Wonder Woman has a completely transparent airplane. But there are degrees, and at high altitude a miss is better than a mile, because the radar sites need precise tracking data. This is exactly what the designers of the Stealth aircraft hope to deny them by introducing just enough fuzziness to degrade the radar system to ineffectuality.

When the radar signature goes down the effectiveness of ECM goes way up, and it's reasonable to believe the Stealth aircraft, though not invisible, *are* immune from attack by most contemporary radar missiles. So at the very least, the Soviet Union will have to spend billions on new radar installations to counter the Stealth aircraft. These new radars would have to be fixed sites—the nature of radar means the bigger the antenna the greater the resolution, and no contemporary mobile radar system could begin to discriminate Stealth aircraft finely enough to do anything about them.

The Stealth penetrators might also find some protection in speed. Modern combat aircraft can only break the sound barrier for brief periods of time because each "supersonic dash" consumes a huge amount of fuel. But future combat aircraft might be able to cruise supersonically "dry"—without using fuel-gulping afterburners—through the use of turbofans of very low bypass ratio. Not only would the "leaky turbojets" allow the new aircraft to operate supersonically four or five times longer than current afterburner-equipped jets, but combined with very high lift-to-drag ratios, the new aircraft might be able to "supercruise"—fly a long range hi-hi-hi mission profile supersonically. (Shades of the B-70! Maybe the Foxbat designers had the right idea all along.)

The new aircraft won't be much of a dogfighter, not in the conventional sense. In the future, air-to-air missiles will take over much of the prepositioning and target acquisition currently performed by the plane and pilot. New developments in microelectronics and small engine technology will give the new missiles longer range, better maneuverability, and the kind of "fire and forget" capability sorely needed in today's air combat arena.

There's no telling when this latest generation of American combat aircraft will become operational, or even if they'll be deployed in Europe—Stealth aircraft may be based in the American desert and flown to their deployment bases aboard huge C-5A transports.

Both East and West have deployed and retired whole generations of fighters in central Europe without firing a shot. Hopefully, even the Stealth aircraft will come and go in peace, like the matched pairs of rival fighters before. Predicting war is a chancy business, even for a man as visionary as Albert Einstein. Someone once asked him if he could predict the kinds of weapons that would be used in World War III. Einstein said no, but "I can assure you, World War IV will be fought with stones."

For some reason, American politicians seem to think of conventional weapons as relatively harmless, especially when compared to nuclear devices. And a conventional war, they think, would be more easily confined to Europe. This is the sort of loose talk that caused France to pull out of NATO and that angers our European NATO allies. They resent being treated as an American firebreak, resent the kind of thinking that envisions a conventional central European war as inevitable, even welcome if it can forestall a worldwide nuclear holocaust.

The Europeans—and especially the Germans—have a right to be apprehensive about American loose talk and sabre-rattling. After all, given the capabilities of modern "conventional" weapons—fuel air explosives, cluster bombs, and chemical and biological munitions—Europe would surely be as scarred and wasted as in any tactical nuclear exchange. And in any "conventional" war it is *their* forests that will be incinerated, *their* rivers poisoned, *their* cities turned into the sauce of civilization. It is all well and good to dare the Russkies to cross the line when you're watching the war on color TV in Cleveland, Ohio. But it is quite another thing to live in, say, Fulda, or Kassel, staring down the actual barrel of a real T-72 tank.

At one time the Americans espoused a strategy of trading cities for time, sound military doctrine considering the limited number of NATO land assets and the limited Soviet resupply capability. But the idea of trading German cities for time didn't appeal too much to the Germans, so now NATO follows the doctrine of "Forward Defense," stopping the assault at the border. It is less practical from a military point of view, but much more acceptable to the German people.

The Europeans believe talking about winning a tactical nuclear war—or even a conventional one—somehow makes the idea of war more possible, and perhaps they are correct. There has certainly been more jingoistic talk coming from the United States in the last couple of years than in any period since the Vietnam War. Some of it has to do with the Soviet buildup, but a lot of it seems to come from a sense of frustration and powerlessness that stems from the stagnation of the American economy and from a confusion of values. As General Sir Ian Hamilton, commander of the British army at Gallipoli, said, "Once in a generation, a mysterious wish for war passes through the people. Their instinct tells them there is no other way of progress and escape from the habits that no longer fit them."

To be fair, the Soviets *are* more dangerous these days, not simply because they've got more tanks and airplanes and the rest of the furniture of war but because they suffer from the same malaise that America has contracted. They've got it even worse—their economy is hopelessly constipated, their leadership old, corrupt, and inbred. They are besieged by hostile nations outside their borders and hostile nationalities within.

The Soviets have always been opportunistic and paranoid but never irrational. They can add up

budgets and fire tubes with the best in the West and could always be counted upon not to do anything stupid. But that's no longer a certainty. Their current leadership cannot last much longer. A new class of Soviet leaders is entering the highest ranks; unable to grasp firsthand the horror of World War II and teethed on the propaganda of Soviet martial invincibility, they too may see war as the only way out of habits that no longer fit them.

But war in central Europe is far from inevitable. East has faced West there for two generations. There have been times of tension but never any overt hostilities. Whether this is because of NATO is hard to say. As one USAFE colonel puts it: "In our culture, what we're trying to do is *not* to fight. Maybe we've done a super job here in Europe for thirty years because nothing's happened—but it's a hard thing to sell to people."

Pilots are not diplomats and perhaps it isn't fair to ask their views on foreign policy. But it is significant that, of all the USAFE pilots we talked to, not *one* said they seriously believed there would be a war in central Europe in the next ten years. Some said maybe in twenty years. Some said there could be a war in another part of the globe. But *no* USAFE serviceman, from crew chief to wing commander, when asked in candor and confidentiality, said he believed World War III—the one you read about so often these days—would take place in the next decade. And for all the aggressiveness bred into the fighter pilots, they are all relieved to say it.

Perhaps their presence makes war less likely. Perhaps deterrence *is* a viable doctrine and not, as one Soviet official puts it, "a concept of 'peace built on terror' which will always be an unstable and bad peace." At any rate, the United States has gone too far with deterrence to back out now. USAFE has been ready for the next world war since the last one. There is no end in sight.

The words of Albert Einstein again come to mind: "I never think about the future," he said. "It comes soon enough."

Appendix
Birdwatchers' Guide to USAFE

USAFE Aircraft Markings

Almost every USAFE tactical aircraft carries a short symbolic history of its origin on its tail. Starting at the top, there is a "fin-flash," or "tail-header," a horizontal bar of color denoting the squadron to which the aircraft is assigned. The fin-flashes are absent from many of the newer aircraft, victims of the Air Force's new emphasis on low-visibility paint schemes.

Underneath the fin-flash there will often be a service badge. The Tactical Air Command likes to put their shield on their aircrafts' tails, but the USAFE badge is almost never carried. Instead, USAFE aircraft usually sport their wing badge on the right intake and their squadron badge on the left. There will always be, however, a tail-code, a two-letter acronym for the aircraft's base.

Under the two letters are a series of numbers: the two digits below the letters *AF* denote the fiscal year in which that particular plane was procured by the Air Force. The larger numbers to the right are the last three digits of the aircraft's serial number. The tail-code on the older planes was white, but now the standard is black letters and numbers, for lower contrast.

Where to See USAFE Planes

USAFE aircraft are frequent visitors to many ranges throughout Europe. Bardenas-Reales in Spain and Aviano in Italy are popular bombing ranges, as are Grafenwöhr, Siegenburg, Baumholder, and Sennelager in Germany and Wainfleet and Spadeadam in England. Fighter pilots like to hassle it out in mock dogfights over water, where there are fewer training restrictions—the North Sea east of Alconbury is a good spot—but the pilots' favorite is the Air Combat Maneuvering Range at Decimommannu, off the west coast of Sardinia.

USAFE aircraft show up all over Europe. It is not uncommon to spot American aircraft at other NATO bases on exchange visits. Neither is it unusual to see USAFE planes at each other's bases. Current wartime plans call for air reinforcements from the United States to deploy not only to USAFE bases, but to other NATO bases as well, especially RAF bases in the United Kingdom and Luftwaffe bases in southern and northern Germany. Under the Colocated Operating Bases (COB) program, USAFE aircraft and reinforcements from the United States would be dispersed

to various Allied airfields in time of war. For example, American F–15 units would be co-located with Canadian, German, and Danish units at Lahr, Soellingen, Berngarten, and Aalborg. USAFE flights in peacetime are often diverted to other NATO bases as a result of bad weather or an in-flight emergency. And USAFE aircraft are also frequent visitors to the large commercial airports.

MAC and SAC Operations in Europe

Although USAFE is a tactical command, it is supported by "heavies" from SAC and MAC. The Strategic Air Command supervises its European

The immense Lockheed C-5A, the world's largest aircraft, at the MAC terminal, Ramstein. Proposals to purchase used commercial Boeing 747s might jeopardize USAF procurement of the improved C-5B version.

operations through its 7th Air Division, headquartered at Ramstein; the Military Airlift Command maintains a similar arrangement, with units falling under its European jurisdiction getting their orders from the 322nd Airlift Division, also at Ramstein. MAC and SAC personnel are permanently assigned to Europe and England for support oper-

133

ations, but the aircraft and aircrews are almost always on temporary duty from the United States and rotate continuously in and out of the European theater.

Although SAC B-52s occasionally deploy to such bases as RAF Marham for exercises, the Strategic Air Command's contribution to USAFE is usually limited to reconnaissance and tanker operations. Most SAC European operations stage out of RAF Mildenhall, which is also the headquarters of USAFE's 3rd Air Force.

Built in 1934, Mildenhall was a key base for RAF Bomber Command during World War II. The Americans arrived in 1950, in the form of the 513th Tactical Airlift Wing, flying cargo aircraft.

The 513th is still at Mildenhall, but is now concerned only with supporting and maintaining the four EC-135 airborne command and control aircraft stationed there for the use of USCINCEUR, the U.S. Commander in Chief, Europe. Crammed with sophisticated electronic communications gear, the Silk Purse aircraft are operated by SAC's 10th Airborne Command and Control Squadron and have been at Mildenhall for almost twenty years.

In terms of numbers, the most important aircraft at Mildenhall are the KC-135 tankers of SAC's 306th Strategic Wing. There are usually around fifteen such aircraft stationed at the base, although the number can double during Crested Cap. As part of the European Tanker Task Force (ETTF), the KC-135s at Mildenhall are charged with the vital task of refueling USAFE tactical aircraft in flight. Until 1979, Mildenhall was the sole operating base of the ETTF; since then, USAFE has re-opened RAF Fairford, Gloucestershire, and established there the 11th Strategic Group, a SAC tanker unit, to relieve some of the pressure on Mildenhall. The 306th also maintains two detachments, the first at Zaragoza, Spain, and the second at Athens, Greece, to refuel USAFE aircraft deployed in the area. The new KC-10 "Extender"

tanker-cargo aircraft, derived from the commercial DC-10, is now making appearances with the ETTF.

The English (indeed, most Europeans) are fanatical aviation buffs—"tail spotters"—and regularly flock to the cyclone fence next to the Mildenhall runway, hoping to catch a glimpse of some rare "bird" with their ever-present cameras and binoculars.

Their patience is often rewarded in the form of such publicity-shy aircraft as the RC-135 electronic surveillance planes of the 306th SW (Strategic Wing) on TDY (temporary duty) from SAC's 55th Strategic Reconnaissance Wing (SRW) at Offutt AFB, Nebraska. E-3A Sentries from the 552nd AWACS Wing at Tinker AFB, Oklahoma, and U-2Rs and SR-71s from SAC's 9th SRW in Beale AFB, California, also put in an occasional visit to Mildenhall. The AWACS regularly deploy to Iceland; the spy planes have been known to roost in bases in the eastern Mediterranean.

As a major destination for MAC personnel and cargo flights, Mildenhall boasts a terminal that would be the envy of many commercial airports. Operated by the 627th Military Airlift Support Squadron, the terminal handles regular C-5 and C-141 flights to and from the United States. A companion unit, the 313th Tactical Airlift Group, shuttles cargo to bases throughout USAFE aboard the sixteen C-130s under its command. The aircraft are operated by units on TDY from the United States for seventy-five-day periods, the 313th being, like so many other European MAC and SAC units, purely an administrative and support unit for other outfits deploying to Europe, and having no aircraft of its own.

RAF Woodbridge is the headquarters of MAC's 67th Aerospace Rescue and Recovery Squadron (ARRS), which reports directly to its parent wing, the 39th Aerospace Rescue and Recovery Wing at Eglin Air Force Base, Florida. In addition to its operation at Woodbridge of HC-130 aircraft and

HH–53 helicopters, the 67th ARRS also operates several detachments: Det 2 at Ramstein provides four UH–1Ns to shuttle USAFE brass around the command: Det 9 at Zaragoza operates three UH–1Hs for rescue work; and Det 14 performs a similar mission at Keflavík, Iceland, with three HH–53s.

Although SAC operations in Germany are negligible, MAC maintains a large presence throughout the 17th Air Force. At Rhein-Main, MAC's 435th Tactical Airlift Wing supports three squadrons: The 37th Tactical Airlift Squadron flies twenty C–130s on supply missions throughout the command. The 55th Aeromedical Airlift Squadron operates four C–9 Nightingales, a special medical version of the civilian DC–9 airliner. The unit was in the spotlight when two Nightingales from Rhein-Main carried the Iranian embassy hostages from Algeria to Germany in 1981, but their regular mission is to link the various hospitals throughout USAFE. The 435th's other unit, the 7111th Operations Squadron, operates a conventionally configured C–9 for VIP missions.

A similar MAC organization, the 58th Military Airlift Squadron at Ramstein, operates a larger fleet of smaller jet transports—a VC–135, five VC–140 Jetstars, seven CT–39 Sabreliners, and three C–12 Super King Airs—for the use of Ramstein's bigger brass.

USAFE Standby and Support Bases

USAFE maintains a group of support bases that have no Air Force aircraft assigned to them but rather accommodate aircraft deployed from other bases. Two of these are in Germany: Lindsey Air Station, operated by the 7100th Air Base Group (ABG), and Tempelhof Central Airport, maintained by the 7350th ABG in West Berlin.

The majority of the USAFE support bases are around the Mediterranean and operate under 16th Air Force command. Aviano Air Base, in northeastern Italy, just south of the Italian Alps, is a favorite stop for rotational USAFE aircraft. Aviano is operated by the 40th Tactical Group. Farther south is San Vito Air Station, run by the 7275th ABG.

There are two USAFE support bases in Greece: Hellenikon, maintained by the 7206th ABG, and Iráklion, on the island of Crete. USAFE maintains a strong presence in Turkey through its TUSLOG headquarters at Ankara, with units at Izmir and Incirlik, a particularly important base for rotational deployments.

Three 3rd Air Force bases in England are "standby deployment bases" kept under care and maintenance by USAFE. These bases could be brought up to operational status in an emergency and are occasionally used in peacetime during training and exercise deployments.

The most noted of these is RAF Greenham Common, Berkshire, site of the famous "Air Tattoo" shows. The base was originally scheduled to be the second location for the European Tanker Task Force, but protests from the local population led to RAF Fairford being chosen instead. RAF Greenham Common is maintained by the 7273rd Air Base Group.

RAF Sculthorpe, Norfolk, is maintained by Det 1 of RAF Lakenheath's 48th Tactical Fighter Wing, and would presumably be used as a satellite base or a base for reinforcements from the United States in times of crisis. RAF Wethersfield, in Essex, is maintained by Det 1 of the 10th Tactical Reconnaissance Wing and serves a similar purpose. Also stationed at RAF Wethersfield is the 819th Civil Engineering Squadron. Called Red Horse for Rapid Emergency Deployable Heavy Operation Repair Squadron Engineering—surely one of the most tortured acronyms in existence, even for the military—the unit's most important function is to quickly repair runways damaged during an airfield attack.

USAFE Aircraft Markings

BASE	TAIL CODE	WING	SQUADRON	FIN-FLASH	AIRCRAFT
17th Air Force					
Bitburg	BT	36th TFW	22nd TFS	Red	F–15 C/D
			53rd TFS	Yellow	F–15 C/D
			525th TFS	Blue	F–15 C/D
Soesterberg	CR	*	32nd TFS	Red	F–15 C/D
Hahn	HR	50th TFW	10th TFS	Blue	F–16A
			313th TFS	White	F–16A
			496th TFS	Red	F–16A
Ramstein	RS	86th TFW	512th TFS	Yellow	F–4E
			526th TFS	Red	F–4E
Seymour Johnson AFB (dual-based)	SJ	4th TFW	334th TFS	Blue	F–4E
			335th TFS	Green	F–4E
			336th TFS	Yellow	F–4E
Spangdahlem	SP	52nd TFW	23rd TFS	Blue	F–4D
			81st TFS	Yellow	F–4G
			480th TFS	Red	F–4E
Zweibrücken	ZR	26th TRW	38th TFS	Green	RF–4C
16th Air Force					
Torrejón	TJ	401st TFW	612th TFS	Blue	F–4D
			613th TFS	Yellow	F–4D
			614th TFS	Red	F–4D

*Reports to Holland for operational control

3rd Air Force

Alconbury	AR	10th TRW	1st TRS	Blue	RF–4C
Lakenheath	LN	48th TFW	492nd TFS	Blue	F–111F
			493rd TFS	Yellow	F–111F
			494th TFS	Red	F–111F
			495th TFS	Green	F–111F
Upper Heyford	UH	20th TFW	55th TFS	Blue	F–111E
			77th TFS	Red	F–111E
			79th TFS	Yellow	F–111E
Bentwaters/ Woodbridge	WR	81st TFW	78th TFS		A–10A
			91st TFS		A–10A
			92nd TFS		A–10A
			509th TFS		A–10A
			510th TFS		A–10A
			511th TFS		A–10A

The Author

Michael Skinner is a Washington, D.C. journalist. A former editor and writer for the *Washington Star* and the *St. Petersburg Times,* he is currently at work on two books, a novel and a non-fiction account of Red Flag, the elaborate aerial war games staged over the Nevada desert.

The Photographer

George Hall is a San Francisco photographer specializing in aerial and aviation topics. For this book, Hall photographed USAFE in action on the ground and in the air, in England, Germany, and Spain. Hall is co-author of *The Blimp Book* (Squarebooks), *Working Fire: The San Francisco Fire Department* (Squarebooks), and *The Great American Convertible* (Doubleday). His photos of carrier flying illustrated the 1980 book *CV: Carrier Aviation* (Presidio Press). *Above:* Photographer Hall (right) with Maj. Rod Kelly, 525th TFS, after F-15 photo flight at Bitburg, Germany.